AQA

Psychology
AS and A-level

Exam Notes for
Research Methods

Published by Educationzone Ltd
P.O. Box 56829
London N21 3YA United Kingdom

© 2018 Educationzone Ltd

British Library Cataloguing in Publication Data:
A catalogue record for this publication is available from the British Library.
ISBN 978-1-906468-46-0

For more information:

Visit our website for exam questions and answers, teaching resources, books and much more:
www.psychologyzone.co.uk Email us for further information: info@psychologyzone.co.uk

Contents

Exam Notes for Research Methods

AS LEVEL SPECIFICATION	A LEVEL SPECIFICATION
3.3.2 Research methods Students should demonstrate knowledge and understanding of the following research methods, scientific processes and techniques of data handling and analysis, be familiar with their use and be aware of their strengths and limitations: • Experimental method. Types of experiment, laboratory and field experiments; natural and quasi experiments. • Observational techniques. Types of observation: naturalistic and controlled observation; covert and overt observation; participant and non-participant observation. • Self-report techniques. Questionnaires; interviews, structured and unstructured. • Correlations. Analysis of the relationship between co-variables. The difference between correlations and experiments.	**4.2.3 Research methods** Students should demonstrate knowledge and understanding of the following research methods, scientific processes and techniques of data handling and analysis, be familiar with their use and be aware of their strengths and limitations: • Experimental method. Types of experiment, laboratory and field experiments; natural and quasi experiments. • Observational techniques. Types of observation: naturalistic and controlled observation; covert and overt observation; participant and non-participant observation. • Self-report techniques. Questionnaires; interviews, structured and unstructured. • Correlations. Analysis of the relationship between co-variables. The difference between correlations and experiments. • Content analysis • Case studies
3.2.3.1 Scientific processes • Aims: stating aims, the difference between aims and hypotheses. • Hypotheses: directional and non-directional. • Sampling: the difference between population and sample; sampling techniques including: random, systematic, stratified, opportunity and volunteer; implications of sampling techniques, including bias and generalisation. • Pilot studies and the aims of piloting. • Experimental designs: repeated measures, independent groups, matched pairs. • Observational design: behavioural categories; event sampling; time sampling. • Questionnaire construction, including use of open and closed questions; design of interviews. • Variables: manipulation and control of variables, including independent, dependent, extraneous, confounding; operationalisation of variables. • Control: random allocation and counterbalancing, randomisation and standardisation. • Demand characteristics and investigator effects. • Ethics, including the role of the British Psychological Society's code of ethics; ethical issues in the design and conduct of psychological studies; dealing with ethical issues in research. • The role of peer review in the scientific process. • The implications of psychological research for the economy.	**4.2.3.1 Scientific processes** • Aims: stating aims, the difference between aims and hypotheses. • Hypotheses: directional and non-directional. • Sampling: the difference between population and sample; sampling techniques including: random, systematic, stratified, opportunity and volunteer; implications of sampling techniques, including bias and generalisation. • Pilot studies and the aims of piloting. • Experimental designs: repeated measures, independent groups, matched pairs. • Observational design: behavioural categories; event sampling; time sampling. • Questionnaire construction, including use of open and closed questions; design of interviews. • Variables: manipulation and control of variables, including independent, dependent, extraneous, confounding; operationalisation of variables. • Control: random allocation and counterbalancing, randomisation and standardisation. • Demand characteristics and investigator effects. • Ethics, including the role of the British Psychological Society's code of ethics; ethical issues in the design and conduct of psychological studies; dealing with ethical issues in research. • The role of peer review in the scientific process. • The implications of psychological research for the economy. • Reliability across all methods of investigation. Ways of assessing reliability: test-retest and inter-observer; improving reliability. • Types of validity across all methods of investigation: face validity, concurrent validity, ecological validity and temporal validity. Assessment of validity. Improving validity. • Features of science: objectivity and the empirical method; replicability and falsifiability; theory construction and hypothesis testing; paradigms and paradigm shifts. • Reporting psychological investigations. Sections of a scientific report: abstract, introduction, method, results, discussion and referencing.

AS LEVEL SPECIFICATION	A LEVEL SPECIFICATION
### 3.2.3.2 Data handling and analysis	### 4.2.3.2 Data handling and analysis
Quantitative and qualitative data; the distinction between qualitative and quantitative data collection techniques.	Quantitative and qualitative data; the distinction between qualitative and quantitative data collection techniques.
• Primary and secondary data, including meta-analysis.	• Primary and secondary data, including meta-analysis.
• Descriptive statistics: measures of central tendency – mean, median, mode; calculation of mean, median and mode; measures of dispersion; range and standard deviation; calculation of range; calculation of percentages; positive, negative and zero correlations.	• Descriptive statistics: measures of central tendency – mean, median, mode; calculation of mean, median and mode; measures of dispersion; range and standard deviation; calculation of range; calculation of percentages; positive, negative and zero correlations.
• Presentation and display of quantitative data: graphs, tables, scattergrams, bar charts.	• Presentation and display of quantitative data: graphs, tables, scattergrams, bar charts.
• Distributions: normal and skewed distributions; characteristics of normal and skewed distributions.	• Distributions: normal and skewed distributions; characteristics of normal and skewed distributions.
• Introduction to statistical testing; the sign test.	• Analysis and interpretation of correlation, including correlation coefficients.
	• Levels of measurement: nominal, ordinal and interval.
	• Content analysis and coding. Thematic analysis.
	### 3.2.3.3 Inferential testing
	Students should demonstrate knowledge and understanding of inferential testing and be familiar with the use of inferential tests.
	• Introduction to statistical testing; the sign test.
	• Probability and significance: use of statistical tables and critical values in interpretation of significance; Type I and Type II errors.
	• Factors affecting the choice of statistical test, including level of measurement and experimental design. When to use the following tests: Spearman's rho, Pearson's r, Wilcoxon, Mann-Whitney, related t-test, unrelated t-test and Chi-Squared test.

The writing in red is the additional information you are required to know if you are taking the A Level two-year course (so you need to know all the exam notes in this study book). If you are taking the AS level course, then you only need to learn the information that is written in blue on the specification.

The AQA specification

The exam requires that you are able to:

▶ Describe, identify and apply your knowledge of the different experimental methods.

▶ Give one advantage and two weaknesses associated with each of these different types of experimental methods.

Introduction

Experimental methods are commonly used in psychological research. There are different types of experiments:

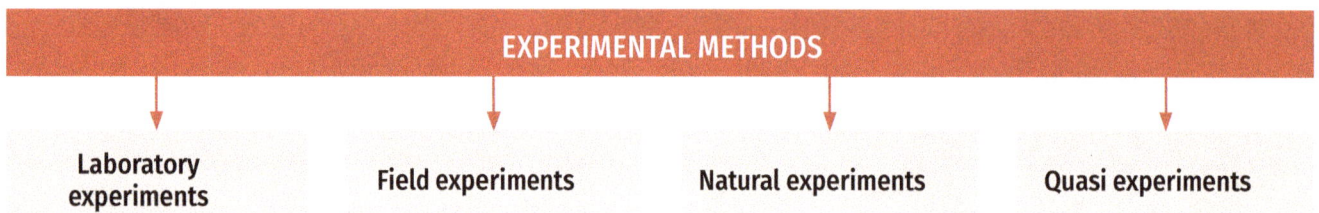

EXPERIMENTAL METHODS

Laboratory experiments	Field experiments	Natural experiments	Quasi experiments

Laboratory experiments

A **laboratory experiment** (or true experiment) is seen as the most scientific psychological method a researcher can use when investigating human behaviour. It is a tightly **controlled** research method conducted in an **artificial environment** in order to test a hypothesis.

The purpose of conducting a laboratory experiment is to see if one variable called the *independent variable (IV)* has an effect on or changes another variable called the *dependent variable (DV)*, with the aim of discovering a **cause-and-effect relationship** (or causal relationship) between the two variables, that is, the change in the IV has an effect on the DV.

The three main characteristics of a laboratory experiment therefore are:

- **Manipulation of the independent variable** – The experimenter manipulates the first variable, the IV to observe what affect it has on the second variable, the DV.

- **Experimental control** – The experimenter ensures, as far as possible, that all other unwanted factors (variables) are controlled (held constant or eliminated). These potential unwanted variables are known as extraneous variables.

- **Randomisation** – A laboratory experiment allows the researcher to randomly allocate the participants to the different experimental conditions.

Independent and dependent variables

An important feature of experimental research is what we call **variables**. In a simple psychology experiment there are usually two variables; the **independent variable (IV)** and the **dependent variable (DV)**. The IV is the one that is *manipulated* and the DV is the one that is *measured* by the experimenter. To understand the difference let us take this hypothesis:

Independe variables

Depende variables

Being hungry has an effect on memory recall

- **Independent variable (IV)** – This is the variable that is **manipulated** by the experimenter to see what effect it has on the *dependent* variable. In the example above, *hunger* would be our independent variable. In a research experiment, a group of participants went without food for a day (i.e. the *hungry* lot = the experimental group). The other group of participants had eaten (i.e. the *not-hungry* lot = control group). The two groups can be compared to see what effect hunger has on memory recall (e.g. remembering words). This is what is meant by manipulating the independent variable (i.e. anything that can be varied such as behaviour, items, events, sizes or amounts).

- **Dependent variable (DV)** – This is the variable that is **measured** (a result or score) by the experimenter. We measure the effects that the independent variable may have on the dependent variable. In our example above, memory recall would be our DV because we are measuring how good memory recall is (e.g. the number of words remembered) when someone is hungry or not hungry.

Experimental control

In order to establish a cause-and-effect relationship between hunger and memory, the experimenter must *control* – or *eliminate* – other 'interfering variables' known as **extraneous variables (EV)** that may influence the participant's memory recall.

Extraneous variables can be defined as any *unwanted* variable (other than the IV) that may potentially affect the results (DV) of the study. If an extraneous variable does affect the results, then we say it has confounded (confused) the results. This is known as a **confounding variable (CV)** and it describes a factor in the experiment that was *not* controlled and that affected the research findings. If this occurs, it reduces the validity of the results, which means we can't trust the research findings. Note that some CVs are easier to identify than others!

Two main types of extraneous variables that can affect the validity of an experiment are:

- **Participant variables** – These refer to individual differences and behaviours of the participants themselves that could influence the results of the experiment, such as age, intelligence, gender, ethnicity, social class, experiences, skills, tiredness, mood and motivation. They can all (unintentionally) influence the outcome of the results. This is only an issue if the experimental design is an *independent group design*. *(See Exam Notes 10)*

- **Situational variables** – These relate to the situational setting of the research, which may affect the participants' behaviour. There might be *environmental factors*, such as the instructions given, the material used, noise levels or temperature, light level and time of day and even weather conditions! Situational variables could also be features of the experiment that leads participants to behave in a particular way called *demand characteristics* and *investigator effect (See Exam Notes 13)*. There is also the *order effect*, whereby the type of *experimental design* can affect the results of the research *(See Exam Notes 2)*.

Example of a study with extraneous variables
In the above example on hunger and memory, the potential situational and participant EVs could be the number of hours they slept the night before the test, their intelligence, and the time of day the test was taken. Let's say we tested the participants at different times of the day, perhaps one group in the morning and the other in the afternoon – the results would then be confounded (i.e. confused). We cannot be sure if the IV (hunger) or the time of day (EV) was the cause of any difference in memory scores among the participants. The time of day would be a confounding variable.

Experimental groups and the control group
In order to see if the IV has an effect on the DV, an experiment must have at least *two groups* (conditions) – one group receives the IV and the other group does not. Then we can compare the results.

- The **experimental** group is exposed to the IV.
- The **control group** is not exposed to the IV.

If the results differ between the two groups, and we have assured ourselves that we have controlled any EVs, then we can conclude that any difference in the participants was due to the IV. For example, in a study on *Revising for an exam while listening to music effects memory recall* :

- The participants in the *experimental group* attempt to learn a psychological theory while listening to music.
- The participants in the *control group* learn a psychological theory without listening to music.

The control group is really important because without them it would be impossible to tell whether the music had any effect on learning. With a control group as a comparison, and if the average score of the experimental group is higher than the average score of the control group, we can conclude that music improves learning. If there were no differences between the groups, then we can conclude that that the IV (listening to music) made no difference.

Randomisation

In the above example, participant EVs would relate to *individual differences*, that is personal characteristics of the participants. It is possible, for example, to assign more participants who are more intelligent to one group than the other. If this occurs, their individual differences will confound the results.

- A way to reduce the effect of personal differences is to use **random assignment** (or randomisation). This is based on the laws of chance. This means that the participants have equal chance of being selected *either* in the experimental group or in the control group.

- The process of *random sampling* (e.g. tossing a coin or running a computer program to generate random numbers) for each participant will determine which group they go into. This means that any personal differences of the participants would be to some extent equally balanced out between the two groups, and this will increase the internal validity of the study.

✓✗ Evaluation

✓ **High levels of control.**
A laboratory experiment allows a high level of control over the research environment. This is done by controlling EVs, which means that the researcher can be confident about establishing a *causal* relationship between the IV and the DV.

✓ **High in reliability.**
Laboratory experiments are easier to replicate than many other research methods. This means that the original experiment can be repeated by other researchers, under the same conditions and following the same procedures, to see whether they obtain similar results. The ability to be replicated is important for checking other researchers' work. If the findings are similar, we can be confident that the original results have internal validity and reliability.

✗ **Artificiality.**
Laboratory experiments have been criticised for being highly artificial, that is they lack mundane realism (because it is not like real-life setting). This means that the results obtained in a laboratory experiment may not be valid because they bear little resemblance to the real world. Therefore research findings from laboratory experiments are difficult to generalise to the real world.

> ✗ **Demand characteristics.**
>
> In a laboratory experiment the participants may show demand characteristics because they know they are taking part in the experiment. Participants naturally will be curious and try to guess what the study is about. Any features of the experiment (e.g. tasks, resources, equipment, video clips), and from the experimenter themselves will act as a clue to what the study maybe about. The participants may unconsciously respond to such cues and will then change their behaviour. This will affect the validity of the findings, because the participants are not behaving as they normally would.

Field experiments

Sometimes experiments are not carried out in an artificial laboratory setting, but in a **real-life environment** where people are in engaged in everyday normal behaviour. Experiments might be conducted in schools or shopping malls, or on the streets or in a workplace. Often, the participants do not know they are taking part in a study. Such experiments are called **field experiments**. In field experiments, the researcher is still able to manipulate the IV in a natural setting, to see the effect it has on the DV.

Example of a field experiment

Sissons (1979) investigated the effect that social class can have on 'helping behaviour' from strangers (helping others out). The confederate (an actor) stood outside Paddington rail station in London and asked people for directions to Hyde Park. In the first part of the experiment the actor was dressed professionally, in a suit and wearing a bowler hat, and he spoke with a middle-class accent. In the other half of the experiment, he changed his clothes into those of a working class labourer and spoke in a working-class accent. He asked passers-by the same question as before. The findings indicated that people were more helpful towards the man who was smartly dressed, with a middle-class accent, than the labourer, implying that people's perception of each other can alter their responses – in this case, how helpful they were.

✓✗ Evaluation

> ✓ **Ecological validity.**
>
> Field experiments are conducted in the real world, where the participants are often not aware they are taking part in a study, so there is no influence of the experimenter effect or demand characteristics. This means that findings of field experiments are often more realistic and true to life than laboratory experiments, and therefore they are high in ecological validity. Therefore findings from field experiments can be generalised to the real world – something laboratory experiments cannot.

> ✗ **Lack of control of variables.**
>
> A problem with field experiments is that the researcher has less control over the natural environment. This means that any unwanted variables (EVs) may be influencing the DV rather than the IV. This reduces the ability to establish a cause-and-effect relationship, which reduces the validity of the research findings.

> ✗ **Issue of reliability.**
>
> Field experiments are less reliable than laboratory experiments, because they are carried out in a natural environment where it is difficult to replicate the study under conditions that are the same as the original. This makes the findings from different field experiments difficult to compare.

✗ Ethical issues.

Field experiments have ethical weaknesses. If the participants are unaware they are taking part in a study, this means they have not agreed to take part (lack of informed consent). In such instances, the researchers should, if possible, attempt to debrief the participant. This means telling the participants at the end of the study, the purpose of the experiment, to reassure them that the information collected will be kept confidential, and have the right to withdraw the data collected on them to be destroyed (if they were not happy being part of the research!).

Natural experiments

Natural experiments, like field experiments, are carried out in a **real-life environment**. The difference is that in a natural experiment the researcher cannot manipulate the IV (whereas in a field experiment they can). All the researcher can do is *observe* a **naturally occurring event** (which is the IV) and measure the naturally occurring effects it produces (the DV). The researcher often looks at data taken *before* and *after* the naturally occurring event and compares them.

Natural experiments are referred to as **quasi-experiments** rather than true experiments, because the researcher cannot manipulate the IV and cannot randomly allocate the participants into different experimental conditions, like in a true experiment.

Example of a natural experiment

Charlton et al. (2002) investigated whether increased exposure to media such as the television increases antisocial behaviours like aggression. He studied a small island called St Helena (a remote island in the South Atlantic Ocean) where television was introduced to the island only recently – in 1995 – to see whether levels of aggression had increased. After five years of television viewing, there was no increase in the children's physical or verbal aggression. Another example of a natural experiment is that by Hodges and Tizard, who studied the effects of privation on children. They wanted to see how privation affects a child's development. To do this, they compared a group of children in institutionalised care with a group of children who were living at home with their families and assessed each child's development (see page 56).

✓✗ Evaluation

✓ Ecological validity.

Natural experiments take place in a natural setting, which means that the results gathered are high in ecological validity. The findings can, therefore, be generalised to similar real-life situations.

✓ Avoid experimenter effects and demand characteristics.

Like field experiments, the participants are unaware that they are taking part in a natural experiment study. This means that their behaviour will be more normal and not subject to experimenter effects and demand characteristics. Again, this increases the ecological validity of the study, which means that the findings can be generalised to the real world.

✓ Only possible method.

Natural experiments allow the psychologists to investigate phenomena that would be impractical or unethical to carry out in a controlled laboratory setting or in a field experiment. For example, a researcher investigating the effects of teenage smoking cannot randomly assign people to groups of smokers and non-smokers to see whether they develop cancer (for obvious ethical reasons!).

✗ Lack of control of variables.

Like field experiments, in natural experiments the researcher has less control over the natural environment. This means that any unwanted variables (EVs) may be influencing the DV rather than the IV. This reduces the ability to establish a cause-and-effect relationship, which reduces the validity of the research findings.

✗ Difficult to replicate.

Natural experiments tend to investigate a phenomenon that is often a unique, one-off situation. This makes it extremely difficult to verify the research findings because it is extremely unlikely that a researcher can replicate the study using the same setting and conditions. Therefore, it is difficult to check the reliability and validity of the results.

Quasi experiments

There are some studies that resemble a true experiment, whereby the IV seems to be manipulated in a controlled setting in which the extraneous variables are held constant. However, they may have share similar characteristics of a true experiment design, but they are not. These are known as **quasi experiments.** Difference between true experiments and quasi-experiments:

In a true experiment, the IV is manipulated in a control way; the participants have an equal chance of being randomly assigned to either the experimental groups, whereas in a quasi-experiment, the participants are not assigned randomly into into the different groups. The experimenter does manipulate the IV.

The reason why participants cannot be randomly allocated to the experimental/control group is because in a quasi experiment the IV is already established and cannot be manipulated. If the IV is gender, age or ethnicity this obviously cannot be changed by the experimenter for the purpose for the experiment. Usually this happens when the independent variable in question is something that is an innate characteristic of the participants involved. This also means natural experiments are deemed as quasi-experiments.

Example

An experimenter wants to see the difference in the reliability of memory recall of female and male participants after watching a crime scene, the researcher cannot manipulate the sex of the participants to randomly allocate them either to be male or female (remember the IV will be the sex; of the participants and DV will be the reliability of information recalled). Female and males are simply assigned to one group or the other – depending whether they are male or female (this is the pre-existing variable).

A psychologist wants to see if personality traits 'extrovert' and 'introvert' has on intelligence. The personality factors are the independent variable. Personality traits are inherent to each person, so random assignment cannot be used. Participants would initially be assigned to one of the groups based on their personality assessment scores.

✓✗ Evaluation

Strength

✓ Comparison can be made.

It allows us to study the effects of variables the psychologists are interested where they cannot manipulate or change the behaviour such as sex, ethnicity etc. This allows comparison between different types of people or behaviours to be made.

Limitation

✓ **Cause-effect relationship cannot be inferred.**
Because in a quasi-experiment there is no random allocation, this means there is no control over the participants. This means that individual differences (social background, IQ, education, experience etc.) leaves open the possibility this might explain the difference in the results between the experimental groups, therefore we cannot be confident in inferring a cause and effect relationship.

Exam Questions

1. Explain what is meant by the term 'laboratory experiment'. . . . . **(2 marks)**

2. Give one advantage of using laboratory experiments in psychological research. . . . . **(2 marks)**

3. Give two weaknesses of using laboratory experiments in psychological research. . . . . **(2+2 marks)**

4. Explain what is meant by the term 'field experiment'. . . . . **(2marks)**

5. Give one advantage of using field experiments in psychological research.. . . . . **(2 marks)**

6. Give two weaknesses of using field experiments in psychological research. . . . . **(2+2 marks)**

7. Explain what is meant by the term 'natural experiment'. . . . . **(2 marks)**

8. Give one advantage of using natural experiments in psychological research. . . . . **(2 marks)**

9. Give two weaknesses of using natural experiments in psychological research.. . . . . **(2+2 marks)**

The AQA specification:

- Experimental designs (independent groups, repeated measures and matched pairs)

The exam requires that you are able to:

▶ Describe, identify and apply your knowledge of the different types of experimental designs.
▶ Give one advantage and two weaknesses of each design (independent groups, repeated measures and matched pairs).

Introduction

Experimental design refers to how individuals will be allocated to each experimental condition (group) when taking part in an experiment. This is important, because there are many ways in which participants can differ from each other, and these differences can act as confounding variables. There are three different ways that participants can be used in experimental design; and each has its advantages and weaknesses. These are:

- Independent group design
- Repeated measures design
- Matched-pairs design.

Independent group design

This means that each participant is *randomly* allocated and tested in *only one* experimental condition. They cannot be in both conditions (group). Look at the following example.

Example of independent group design

Forty participants are taking part in an experiment to test the hypothesis that listening to music affects their memory recall. In an independent group design, the participants will be randomly allocated to one group. So, 20 participants will revise while listening to music (experimental group), while the other twenty will revise without listening to music (control group).

✓✗ Evaluation

✓ **Removes order effect.**

Independent group design avoids the possibility of order effect because participants have taken part in only one condition. Order effect is when the participants take part in both (or all) the conditions, which can effect the participant's responses. There are two types of order effect. There is the **practice effect** whereby any improvement in performance in the second of the two conditions might be due to participants already having had a practise at doing the task in the first condition. Equally, if performance is worsened through doing the experiment twice, this might be due to boredom, which is known as the **fatigue effect**. Either way, this would act as a confounding variable that would effect the validity of the results. Taking part in only one condition eliminates this possibility.

✓ **Reduces demand characteristics.**
Using an independent group design reduces the effect of demand characteristics, because the participants take part in one condition only. Therefore it is less likely that they will guess the purpose of the study. If they take part in more than one condition, they are more likely to guess the aim of the experiment, which may affect their performance.

✗ **Randomisation not guaranteed.**
Even if participants are randomly assigned, we cannot be sure that any individual differences will be balanced out between the two conditions. There is still a possibility that the result may be due to individual differences. For example, when investigating the effect of listening to music on memory, any differences between the two conditions could be due to one group having better memories, on average, or being more intelligent, rather than manipulation of the IV (the music).

✗ **More participants needed.**
Independent group design requires more participants – twice as many as a repeated measures design experiment.

Repeated measures design
With a repeated measures design, the same participants take part in both (or all) of the conditions in the experiment.

Example of repeated measures design.
If we take the previous example of music and memory recall, in a repeated measures design the same participants (all 40 of them) would be used in both conditions. First, they would revise while listening to the music (experimental condition), then they would revise without listening to the music (control group).

✓✗ Evaluation

✓ **Eliminates individual differences.**
Repeated measures design eliminates the possibility of individual differences (e.g. variations in intelligence, experience, motivation), because the same people's performances are measured in both conditions and are therefore held constant.

✓ **Fewer participants are needed.**
Half as many participants are needed for a repeated measures design.

✗ **Possibility of order effect.**
Repeated measures design increases the possibility of order effects if the participants experience both conditions.

✗ **Increases demand characteristics.**
Using a repeated measures design increases the possibility of demand characteristics. Because the participants take part in two conditions there is a likelihood that they will guess the aim of the study, and this is likely to affect their performances.

- ## Counterbalancing (dealing with order effect and demand characteristics)

One way to minimise order effect and demand characteristics in repeated measures design is by **counterbalancing**. This is when participants are divided equally between the experimental conditions. Half are randomly assigned to be tested in condition A followed by condition B (A → B). The other half are tested in condition B followed by condition A (B → A) – thus AB and BA, or ABBA (just remember the pop group). In this way, the order of the experimental conditions are not the same for everyone, as some will carry out condition B first and some will carry out A first.

Matched-pairs design

Essentially this is the same as independent group design. Different participants are used for each experimental condition, but the participants in both conditions are **matched** according to similar characteristics that are important for that particular study. For example, participants in condition A will be matched with other participants who have similar characteristics (in terms of sex, ethnicity, gender and IQ) who are assigned to condition B.

Example of matched pairs design

If we want to test the hypothesis that IQ level has an effect on memory recall, in a matched pairs design we may select a participant with an IQ of 110, who is 'paired' with another person of the same IQ level. The matched participants are then allocated into the different experimental conditions.

✓✗ Evaluation

✓ **Removes the order effect and demand characteristics.**
A matched pairs design reduces order effect and demand characteristics because there are different participants in each condition.

✓ **Individual differences.**
Individual differences are minimised though pair matching, and thus there is less chance of any variation in the participants across the conditions.

✗ **Twice as many participants are needed.**
A matched pairs design requires twice as many participants, which can be time-consuming, compared to the repeated measure design.

✗ **Matching difficulties.**
It can be extremely difficult to match all the variables between each pair of participants.

Exam Questions

1. A psychologist wanted to investigate whether recall of information is more effective when the context (setting) of the original learning of information is similar at the time of recall. To do this, the researcher asked one group of students to learn and recall a list of 15 words in the same room. The other group of students were tested in a different context, by learning in one room and recalling in another.

    a) What experimental design was used in this study? . . . . **(1 mark)**

    b) Explain one advantage of this experimental design in the context of this study. . . . . **(2 marks)**

    c) Explain one weakness of this experimental design in the context of this study. . . . . **(2 marks)**

The AQA specification:

- Observational techniques. Types of observation: naturalistic and controlled observation; covert and overt observation; participant and non-participant observation.

The exam requires that you are able to:

▶ Describe, identify and apply your knowledge of observational techniques.
▶ Give one advantage and two weaknesses associated with observational techniques.

Naturalistic and controlled observations

Most psychological research uses **observations** as a way of gathering and recording data on humans. The two main types of observations are *naturalistic* observation and *controlled* observation.

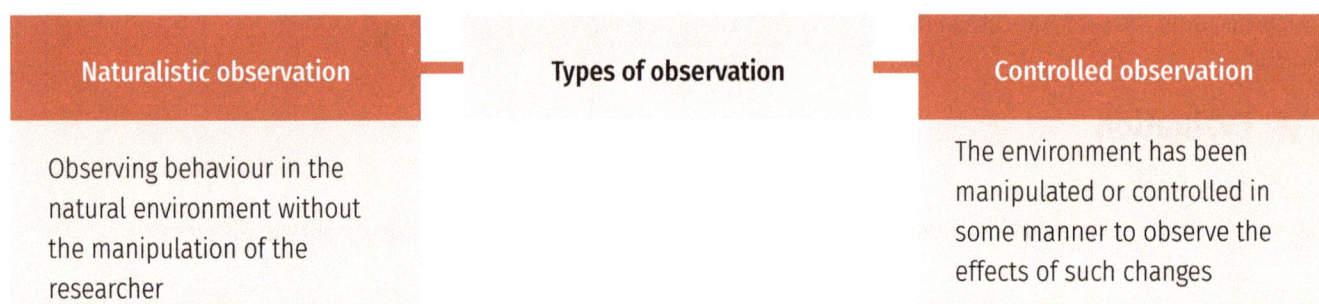

Naturalistic observation	Types of observation	Controlled observation
Observing behaviour in the natural environment without the manipulation of the researcher		The environment has been manipulated or controlled in some manner to observe the effects of such changes

Naturalistic observations

Naturalistic observations involve the researcher observing and collecting data on people's *naturally occurring behaviour* in their *natural environment* without interference or manipulation of the environment. For example, this may take place in a workplace, a hospital ward or a nursery.

Controlled observation

Controlled observations are carried out when the researcher deliberately manipulates or controls the environment in a particular way and observes the effects. For example, Ainsworth (1978) used a controlled observation by bringing children to a laboratory play room and observed and recorded the child's reactions (through a one-way mirror) when separated from the mother, or when introduced to a stranger. The situation was a controlled setting because Ainsworth manipulated the laboratory play room by controlling the behaviour of the mother (having to leave the play room) and the stranger (the appearance of the stranger).

✓✗ Evaluation

Naturalistic observation

✓ **High ecological validity.**
Naturalistic observations achieve a higher level of ecological validity than any other research method, because the subjects being studied are usually unaware and therefore behave as they usually would. This means that participant effects (e.g. demand characteristics) will be prevented, so the findings will be high in validity.

✗ Observer bias.

In naturalistic observations, the researchers may be selective in what they want to see. They unconsciously filter information, accepting only the information that will confirm their hypothesis. Such an unconscious process leads to the data being biased, which will affect the validity of the findings.

✗ Cannot establish cause and effect.

In naturalistic observations, the researcher can only establish a relationship between the two variables that are observed. This is because the researcher has no control over potential EVs. This means that the cause-and-effect relationship between the variables cannot be established with certainty.

✗ Ethical issues.

In naturalistic observations, the participants are unaware that they are being observed, which raises ethical issues regarding invasion of privacy and lack of informed consent. If participants are informed about the observation, there is a very high possibility that they will behave differently (demand characteristics) which will lower the validity of the findings.

Controlled observations

✓ High control of variables.

Controlled observations allow a higher level of control (than naturalistic observations) over possible EVs that may influence the participants' behaviour.

✗ Demand characteristics.

In controlled observations the participants are aware that they are being observed, so there is a high possibility that demand characteristics will occur, which can lower the validity of the research findings.

Observational techniques

Below are some design issues the researcher will need to consider when conducting observational research.

Covert or overt observations

The researcher will need to decide whether the observation is kept 'a secret' from the participants.

- **Covert (undisclosed) observation** is when the researcher does not tell the participants that they are being observed and their real identity is hidden.
- **Overt (disclosed) observation** is when the participants know they are being observed and usually they know the reason why.

Participant and non-participant observation

In observational research, the role of the observer can be either:

- **Non-participant** whereby the researcher merely observes the participants and does not participate in the activity being studied.
- **Participant** whereby the researcher becomes a participant and engages in the activity with those being studied.

Data collection

The researcher will need to decide on how the data will be collected, and whether the observation will be *structured* or *unstructured*.

- **Structured observation** – The observed behaviour is recorded in a systematic and structured manner by using *behavioural categories* (*see Exam Notes* 4). This type of structured observation produces *quantitative* data whereby the information gathered can be put into numerical form (numbers) and can be analysed statistically to see whether there is a relationship between the variables.

- **Unstructured observation** – There are no pre-coded behaviour categories, so the researcher freely writes down random notes on the behaviour they are observing. Unstructured observations produce qualitative data, whereby the information is often presented in descriptive form (written). This provides a deeper and fuller picture of the participant's behaviour, enabling the researcher to get a better understanding of behaviour.

Exam Questions

1. Explain what is meant by the term 'naturalistic observation'. . . . . **(2 marks)**

2. Explain what is meant by the term 'controlled observation'. . . . . **(2 marks)**

3. Give one advantage of using naturalistic observation in psychological research. . . . . **(2 marks)**

4. Give two disadvantages of using naturalistic observation in psychological research. . . . . . . **(2+2 marks)**

5. Give one advantage of using controlled observation in psychological research. . . . . **(2 marks)**

6. Give two disadvantages of using controlled observation in psychological research.. . . . . . . **(2+2 marks)**

7. Identify one ethical issue that may arise from observational research and suggest how this could be dealt with.. . . . . **(3 marks)**

The AQA specification:

- Observational design: behavioural categories; event sampling; time sampling.

The exam requires that you are able to:

▶ Describe the design process of naturalistic observations.
▶ Identify and formulate behavioural categories.

Introduction

You should be familiar with observational methods, as well as the advantages and weaknesses *(see Exam Notes 3)*. The researcher will need to make some decisions about design when conducting observational research. Some of these have already been mentioned in *Exam Notes 3*, they are:

- **The type of observation method** – naturalistic or a controlled observation?

- **The role of the observer** – disclosed or undisclosed? Participant or non-participant observer?

- **Data collection** – structured or unstructured observation?

Design issues for naturalistic observations

One difficultly for the researcher when conducting a naturalistic observation (as well as controlled observation) is *how* to record the data and *what* to record. This will depend on whether the observation is structured or unstructured. For example, if:

Unstructured observation	Structured observation
The observer has no ordered system of collecting data, but merely records the appropriate behaviour when it occurs using:	The observer uses a systematic and structured manner to record the appropriate behaviour when it occurs using:

- Written note taking
- Video recordings
- Audio recordings

- Behavioural categories (plus the help of video and audio recording to help with the anaysis)

- Sampling procedures

Structured observations

Behavioural categories

If a **structured observation** is chosen, the observer (before the study begins) has to decide what types of behaviours are to be recorded. This is achieved by creating **behavioural categories**, which involves designing a grid/table worksheet with separate categories (i.e. columns) in which the different types of behaviour, when they occur, are then recorded in the appropriate category. The behaviour can be recorded in many ways, depending on what is being observed (such as a tally system, rating scale or a coding system).

Before the researcher can create behavioural categories, the behaviour to be observed needs clear **operational definitions** (to be operationalised). This means clearly defining *how* the observed behaviour will be tested and and *how* the behaviour will be measured. For example, to investigate physical aggression in children, the concept *physical aggression* must be operationalised by observing behaviour such as punching, scratching and kicking (the behaviour that is being 'tested' part) and seeing how often this occurs during playtime (the 'measuring' part).

Different ways that behaviour can be recorded

Tally system	Counting the frequency of the behaviour as it occurs	For example, aggressive behaviour in a school playground could be measured by counting the amount of biting, hitting, pulling and wrestling that takes place, as it occurs.
Rating scale	A point scale system of varying intensity	For example, on a 1 to 4 rating scale of helping behaviour for a person in distress: 4 = very helpful; 3 = some help offered; 2 = aware victim needed help but did not offer; 1 = unhelpful and ignored victim.
Coding system	A system that uses letters or numbers to record the observed behaviour	For example, in a coding system for observing peer-play interactions of pre-school children at a nursery: CI = close interaction (children playing closely with each other); H = helping behaviour (children helping other children with a task); W = withdrawn (child not engaged in task or with other children).

Example of behavioural categories for observing aggressive behaviour in children within a playground

Child	Hits or shoves others with force – unprovoked	Hits or shoves others with force – following peers	Hits or shoves others with force – retaliation	Shouts at others – Unprovoked	Shouts at others – following peers	Shouts at others – retaliation
A	⊦⊦⊦⊦ II	⊦⊦⊦⊦	IIII			IIII
B		⊦⊦⊦⊦ III			II	
C		III		IIII		III
D		I	⊦⊦⊦⊦	II		⊦⊦⊦⊦

Adapted source: Cool can, H. (1999) Research Methods and Statistics in Psychology, Second Edition.

Sampling procedures

It is unlikely that the researcher will be able to record all the observed behaviour continuously. One way to record the behaviour is to take a sample during the observation. The three main different sampling techniques for observations are:

- **Event sampling** – This is when the researcher records a particular behaviour whenever it occurs. For example, investigating aggression in a classroom setting, the researcher might record it every time an aggressive event takes place.

- **Time interval sampling** – This is when the whole period of observation is split into time intervals and the behaviour is recorded on a regular basis at specific times. For example, the researcher notes down what an individual is doing every 30 seconds for the whole duration of the observation.

- **Time point sampling** – The researcher makes a record of the observed behaviour at a par- ticular point of time during the period of observation. For example, the researcher may observe children in the playground and record what happens during the first five minutes of playtime and then again during the last five minutes.

Exam Questions

1. A researcher decided to investigate whether children who attend pre-school day-care centre five times a week are more physically aggressive than those who attend twice a week. The researcher carries out a naturalistic observation at his local pre-school day care centre. The children were observed every morning during their outside play period for one hour.

   a) Suggest two suitable behavioural categories that researcher could use to record the children's aggressive behaviour. . . . . **(2 marks)**

   b) How might the researcher record the children's behaviour during the observation? . . . . . . **(2 marks)**

The AQA specification:

- Self-report techniques. Questionnaires; interviews, structured and unstructured.

The exam requires that you are able to:

▶ Describe, identify and apply your knowledge of self-report techniques (questionnaires and interviews).
▶ Give one advantage and two weaknesses associated with self-report techniques.

Introduction

Self-report techniques involve asking participants to provide information about themselves (hence the term *self-report*) on issues such as attitudes, beliefs, opinions and feelings. The two most well-known self-report techniques are *questionnaires* and *interviews* (often referred to as surveys).

Questionnaires

A **questionnaire** can be defined as a **pre-determined set of written questions**. Respondents are invited to fill in their answers and return the questionnaire to the researchers. There are two basic types of questions that can be asked:

- **Closed questions** – These questions come with a range of answers to choose from that must be circled or ticked as appropriate by the respondent. Closed questions are regarded as producing *quantitative* data because the answers collected can be summarised in a numerical form (e.g. to find the mean, mode or median), which makes them easy to analyse and draw conclusions.

- **Open questions** – There are no pre-set answers given to the question, so respondents can freely express themselves however they choose. Open questions produce *qualitative* data because the respondents answers often involve a detailed descriptive account.

Examples of closed and open questions

Closed: Do you think mothers should stay at home and look after their children? (Respondents choose from: Strongly agree / Agree / Disagree / Strongly disagree)
Open: What is your opinion of the latest Harry Potter film? (Respondents answer freely)

✓✗ Evaluation

✓ **Cheap.**
Questionnaires are generally easier, cheaper and quicker to administer (e.g. via email) than other research methods. For example, compared with interviews they are easier to use, the researcher does not need any special training to use them or pay the interviewer's expenses. The lower cost also means that a larger sample of people can be obtained.

✓ **More truthful answers.**
Anonymous questionnaires allow the participants to be more honest with their answers than in a face-to-face interview, especially if there are sensitive or personal issues. The presence of the interviewer may influence the respondents' answers, which will decrease the validity of the data.

✗ Bias response.
Respondents may not answer the questionnaire in a truthful way. They may lie or deliberately give any false answer just to complete the questionnaire as quickly as possible. Or they may provide information that presents them in positive light, or give answers they think should be given, rather than more truthful answers. This is known as social desirability bias and it can decrease the validity of the data.

✗ Low response rate.
Self-completing questionnaires suffer from a low response rate (not many people fill them in or send them back). If the response rate is 25% or less, it may have a critical effect on the results, which will be of very little value if the sample is not representative of the population or group from which the sample was taken. Non-response is also a problem, because the people who do not return questionnaires differ from those who do. Those who do return them tend to be of a higher social group and more educated, thus introducing bias into the results.

✗ Wording of questions.
Questionnaires can only be effective if the questions are sufficiently simple and straightforward to understand. If the words are not understood in the same way by everybody, this will affect how the respondents answer, which may affect the validity of the findings.

Interviews

An **interview**, like a questionnaire, consists of questions. This time they are asked by an interviewer face-to-face. Interviews can be *structured*, *unstructured* or *semi-structured*.

- **Structured interviews:** All the questions and the range of answers are pre-determined, like in a questionnaire. The only difference is that the questions are read out aloud by the interviewer and the respondent answers verbally rather than writing anything down.

- **Unstructured interviews:** The interviewer introduces a number of research topics for discussion, with very few pre-determined questions. The interview is open and flexible so that respondents can express themselves freely and in greater depth, because there are no fixed responses required. The interviewer may raise more questions during the interview based on any information he or she finds interesting.

- Semi-structured interviews: These lie somewhere in-between a structured and an unstructured interview. The researcher has a set of pre-determined questions but can also ask additional questions depending on the respondent's answers, to probe further for more details or clarification or to open up a new line of enquiry. An example of this is a clinical interview in which the interviewer asks pre-determined questions, but follows up with spontaneous questions depending on the responses of the person being interviewed.

✓✗ Evaluation

✓ Deeper understanding.
The flexibility of unstructured and semi-structured interviews allows the researcher to explore and probe deeper into the opinions and attitudes of the respondent, which can provide a rich and in-depth information. This is something that cannot be done with other research methods, such as close-ended questionnaires or experiments.

✓ Good for sensitive subjects.
Interviews are more effective for sensitive subjects than a questionnaire. Having an interviewer who is sympathetic and understanding towards the respondent is more likely to generate a more truthful response.

✗ **Social desirability bias.**

Respondents may give answers that they believe the interviewer wishes to hear. Or they may answer questions in a particular way that portrays them in positive light (social desirability bias) rather than giving a truthful answer. This will affect the validity of the findings.

✗ **Interviewer effect.**

The interviewer may unintentionally influence the participant's responses by such things as wearing particular clothing, making certain gestures, and using a certain tone of voice. Ethnicity, age, and gender can also play a part in influencing the answers given by the respondent.

✗ **Interviewer bias.**

This occurs when the interviewer has a desired expectation or preference about the outcome of the study, so they unintentionally act in a way that may influence the response of the participants. This can also affect how the interviewer interprets the data, making him or her more selective of data that confirms the research hypothesis and more disregarding of data that may not support it. This is usually done without awareness.

Exam Questions

1. Explain the difference between close-ended questionnaires and open-ended questionnaires. . . . **(3 marks)**

2. Give one advantage of using questionnaires in psychological research. . . . . **(2 marks)**

3. Give two weaknesses of using questionnaires in psychological research.. . . . . **(2+2 marks)**

4. Give one advantage of using interviews in psychological research. . . . . **(2 marks)**

5. Give two weaknesses of using interviews in psychological research.. . . . . **(2+2 marks)**

The AQA specification:

- Questionnaire construction, including use of open and closed questions; design of interviews.

The exam requires that you are able to:

▶ Describe the design process of questionnaires and interviews.

Introduction

You should be familiar with self-report methods (questionnaires and interviews) as well as the advantages and weaknesses associated with each one (*see Exam Notes 5*).

Questionnaires

When administering a questionnaire the researcher will need to make decisions on design issues. The type of data the researcher is seeking to gain will determine the format of the questions (e.g. closed questions or open questions). There are two types of data:

- **Quantitative data = closed questions** such as 'Do you think mothers should stay at home and look after the baby?' YES or NO. These produce quantitative data because the answer can be put into numbers. It makes the data easier to analyse and draw a conclusion.

- **Qualitative data = open questions** such as 'Why do you think some mothers are reluctant to employ a nanny?' Open questions produce qualitative data because the respondent's answers consist of words that offer a detailed descriptive account of the particpant's view.

Construction of questions

The researcher needs to ensure that the questions are appropriately worded so that misunderstandings that can otherwise affect the reliability and validity of the data are eliminated. Some things to consider are shown in the list below.

- **Use plain language** – This helps avoid unclear or confusing questions that may be understood differently by different respondents. For example, asking 'How often do you go the pub?' is an ambiguous question because the word 'often' is open to interpretation. This could be replaced with 'How many times do you go to the pub in a week?'

- **Avoid leading/loaded questions** – These questions can affect how a respondent answers. For example, asking 'Don't you think that teachers should be paid more money?' is *leading* because it leads the respondent to answer 'Yes'. *Loaded* questions contain emotive language which may bias the response of the respondent in a particular way. For example, 'Do you think it is right to kill defenceless animals in laboratories, or should it be stopped?'

- **Avoid double-barred questions** – These questions have two possible answers. An example is 'Do you think teachers are tired all the time because they don't get enough sleep or because they drink too much?' This question should be rewritten as two separate questions.

- **Avoid complex questions** – Long and difficult sentences that contain jargon (technical words) should be avoided. For example 'Do you think the rise in psychotic illnesses has been due to the pressure of the individualistic lifestyle people lead now, or has the change in legislation towards psychotic illness been the contributory factor for the increase?'

Interviews

Again, you should be familiar with interview methods as well as the advantages and weaknesses associated with interviews. The researcher will need to consider certain design issues, such as the type of data the researcher is seeking to collect. This will determine the format of the interview. The types of data yielded by an interview are:

- **Quantitative data** – If the researcher is seeking basic information (e.g. Very often, Sometimes, not often or the Yes or No type) where they can quantify the data into numbers and analyse and draw a conclusion from the information collected, then the researcher will opt for **structured interviews** (questions are already determined before hand with set of fixed possible answers).

- **Qualitative data** – If the researcher wants to ask 'Why' questions, to find out about beliefs, opinions and attitudes, for example, then **unstructured** or **semi-structured** interviews (questions and answers are not determined before hand) are favoured. They produce qualitative data because the respondent's answers offer a detailed and descriptive account of the participant's view (although it is difficult to analyse).

- **Construction of questions** – The wording of the questions in interviews is as important as it is for questionnaires, therefore all the issues discussed under 'Construction of questions' also apply to interviews.

Interviewer effect

Conducting an interview means that a high level of interaction between the interviewer and interviewee is expected. This means that the interviewer may unintentionally bias the participant's responses, which is known as the **interviewer effect**, which can affect the validity of the research. In order to minimise bias, the interviewer should:

- Ensure that interviews are standardised.

- Have a formal dress code.

- Express neither approval nor disproval of the answers given by the respondent.

- Be pleasant and sincere.

- Ensure that the questions are asked in a neutral manner (non-emotive).

- Adopt similar personal characteristics.

Adopting similar characteristics is a way to further reduce the interview effect by matching the interviewer and respondents in terms of their personal characteristics. Research studies have shown that the respondent relates better to someone of the same age, gender, ethnicity and social class.

Exam Questions

1. Give one example of a closed question. . . . . **(1 mark)**

2. Give one example of an open question. . . . . **(1 mark)**

3. Outline one design issue that researchers need to consider when constructing a questionnaire. . . **(2 marks)**

4. Outline one design issue that researchers need to consider when constructing an interview (other than the answer you have given for question 3) . . . . **(2 marks)**

The AQA specification:

- Correlations. Analysis of the relationship between co-variables. The difference between correlations and experiments.

The exam requires that you are able to:

▶ Describe, identify and apply your knowledge of correlational analysis.
▶ Recognise and interpret different types of correlation (e.g. positive, negative, correlation coefficients).
▶ Give one advantage and two weaknesses associated with correlational analysis.

Introduction

The term **correlation** refers to the view (or aiming to see) that a relationship exists between two variables in some way. For example, we can say there is 'correlation' between the amount of time students spend on the social networking site Facebook and their exam performance.

Correlation research

The purpose of a correlation research is to see whether there is a relationship between two variables. We can refer to *non-experimental methods* such as interviews, questionnaires and naturalistic observations as being correlational research. This is because the researcher has less control over the research conditions with these methods. The best that the research findings can show is a 'relationship' between the two variables, whereas in a laboratory experiment the researcher can manipulate and control the variables in order to establish a cause-and-effect relationship between them.

Example of correlational research

You may carry out a questionnaire survey to see whether there is a correlation between jealousy and the time a relationships lasts. The more jealous you are, the shorter your relationship may be – or the less jealous you are, the longer your relationship will last.

Correlational analysis

The term **correlational analysis** refers to a mathematical statistical formula used to analyse data from correlational research. The aim is to discover whether a relationship exists between the two variables, that is, the type of relationship the two variables have (positive, negative or zero), and how strong this relationship is between them.

Positive and negative correlation

There are three possible results of a correlational study: a *positive* correlation, a *negative* correlation, or a *zero* correlation. If we have two variables (*x* and *y*), then:

- **Positive correlation** exists when the two variables *increase* or *decrease* together. For example, a high score in variable *x* (e.g. frustration) tends to be associated with a high score in variable *y* (e.g. aggression). We can say that they are positively correlated, meaning that as frustration rises, so do acts of aggression. Equally, because one variable *(x)* decreases, so does the other variable *(y)*.

- **Negative correlation** exists when one variable increases and the other decreases. For example, a high score in variable *x* (the amount of alcohol we drink) is correlated with a low score in variable *y* (the less we can balance on one leg).

- **Zero correlation** is when there is no relationship between the two variables.

Correlational coefficient

A **correlational coefficient** is a numerical value (number) that describes the **strength** and the **type** of relationship that exist between the two variables. The type of relationship can be positive, negative or zero, and the strength, shown by the number, can vary on a scale from +1 to –1 where:

+1   =   perfect positive correlation

–1   =   perfect negative correlation

0   =   zero correlation

A correlation coefficient cannot be greater than +1 or –1

A negative correlation might have a value –0.49, whereas a positive correlation might be +0.82. The plus or minus sign tells us whether it is a positive or negative correlation.

The nearer the coefficient is to +1 or –1, the stronger the relationship is. So, for example, a coefficient of –0.89 shows a strong (but negative) correlation as the number is close to –1 (as one variable increases the other variable decreases), while a coefficient of +0.62 shows a moderate (but positive) relationship between the two variables (as one variable increases so does the other).

In summary
- A correlation coefficient close to +1.00 indicates a strong positive correlation.
- A correlation coefficient close to –1.00 indicates a strong negative correlation.
- A correlation coefficient of 0 indicates that there is no correlation.

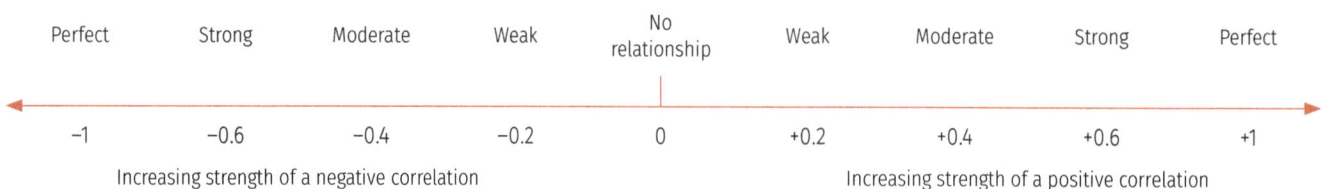

Perfect	Strong	Moderate	Weak	No relationship	Weak	Moderate	Strong	Perfect
–1	–0.6	–0.4	–0.2	0	+0.2	+0.4	+0.6	+1

Increasing strength of a negative correlation   Increasing strength of a positive correlation

Scattergrams (scattergraphs) are used to display correlational data visually.
They are covered in more detail in Exam Notes 21.

✓✗ Evaluation

> ✓ **The difference between experiments and correlations.**
> In an experiment, the researcher manipulates the IV and records the effects of the DV. By doing this, a cause-and-effect relationship can be demonstrated. In a correlation there is no manipulation of the variables (IV), and so cause-and-effect cannot be demonstrated. This is because the influence of extraneous variables has not controlled, so it may be that a third variable, that has not been accounted for causing the relationship between the co-variables (often called the 'intervening variable').

✓ **When experimentation is not possible.**

Correlational research is used when it would be unethical or inappropriate to investigate human behaviour under experimental conditions. For example, it would be unethical to carry out an experiment to see whether smoking causes lung cancer (we could not make people smoke themselves to death!). Instead, a questionnaire or an interview may be used and the data analysed to see whether a relationship between the two variables exists. This is far more acceptable and ethical.

✓ **Naturally occurring variables.**

Correlational research is able to study the relationship between two variables that occur naturally in society – for example, exam stress and students getting ill.

✓ **Further research.**

Correlational analysis is useful as it can identify whether a relationship exist or not between the two variables. If a relationship does exist, it can lead to experiments to see whether a causal relationship may be established.

✗ **No cause and effect.**

Correlational analysis does not establish a cause-and-effect relationship between the two variables – that is, that one variable has caused a change in the other variable. This is because there may be other factors involved. For example, a correlational analysis may show a relationship between violent video games and aggressive behaviour in young children, but this could also be due to another influence such as marital conflict in the home, or divorce, or parenting style. For example, if the parents tend to be aggressive or violent themselves, this will be seen by the child as acceptable behaviour. The uncertainly surrounding correlational evidence reduces the validity of the findings.

✗ **Ineffective curvilinear relationships.**

Correlational analysis is only effective for linear (straight-line) relationship between the two variables – but not for a nonlinear relationship (such as curvilinear ones). For example, the relationship between environmental temperature and aggression may initially show a positive correlation, because as temperature rises, so does aggressive behaviour. But this is only true up to a certain point. When the temperature becomes very high, aggressive behaviour drops and so the relationship, becomes a negative one. This kind of relationship is called a curvilinear relationship (inverted U-relationship e.g. ⌒). If we calculate the correlation coefficient of the curvilinear relationship it tends to show a zero correlation, even though this is clearly not the case. This shows that using correlational coefficients can be deceptive in terms of the type of relationship between the two variables, as demonstrated by curvilinear relationships.

Exam Questions

1. Explain what is meant by the term 'correlation coefficient'. . . . . (**2 marks**)

2. A correlation coefficient in a study was found to be −0.84. Explain what this indicates. . . . . . . (**2 marks**)

3. Give one advantage of using correlational analysis in psychological research. . . . . (**2 marks**)

4. Give two weaknesses of using correlational analysis in psychological research. . . . . (**2+2 marks**)

The AQA specification:

A-LEVEL ONLY

- Content analysis and coding.
- Thematic analysis

The exam requires that you are able to:

▶ Describe ways in which qualitative data can be analysed and interpreted.
▶ Analyse and interpret qualitative data that is presented in the exam.

Qualitative research methods

Qualitative data refers to data that is collected in descriptive form – meaning in written words (or audio and video material) rather than as numbers such as scores. The purpose of gathering qualitative data is to provide a rich and detailed account of the participants' meanings, thoughts and experiences, thus allowing a deeper understanding into human behaviour.

Research methods that collect qualitative data (or qualitative research methods) are:

- **Naturalistic (unstructured) observations** (e.g. diary notes, audio/video recordings)
- **Unstructured interviews** (e.g. interview transcriptions where the interviewed conversation is transferred from audio into a written form)
- **Open-ended questionnaires** (e.g. respondents can answer the set of questions freely).

Presentation of qualitative data

Just like quantitative data, researchers need to **analyse** qualitative data to enable them to draw a conclusion. This can be challenging to do as qualitative data often produces a wealth of material, making it difficult to make sense of what the material may suggest. One way to present qualitative data is to **summarise** the material in a meaningful way. This can be done through the process of **categorisation** by applying:

- **Content analysis** – This involves converting qualitative data into numbers (i.e. quantitative data).
- **Thematic analysis** – This involves analysing qualitative data for themes and presenting it in written form (still remains in qualitative form).

Content analysis

Content analysis, as the name suggests, is a technique used to 'analyse' the 'content' of qualitative data. The purpose of content analysis is to summarise a large of amount of written material by converting it into numbers. Content analysis is often used to evaluate media such as TV programmes, advertisements, magazines, video recordings and transcripts of interviews from psychological research.

Design process of content analysis

Content analysis will need careful planning by the researcher. Just like any other research design, there are stages to follow:

| Research question/ hypothesis | → | Sample | → | Categories | → | Piloting | → | Analyse & present |

- **Research question/hypothesis** – You will need to formulate a research question or a hypothesis. This should clearly state the specific question or a statement of prediction (hypothesis) you wish to research. For example, 'Is there a difference in the subject matter devoted to the front cover of male and female magazines?'

- **Sampling** – Select the sample material that is representative of the topic of interest to be analysed (e.g. which magazines). Consider the *quantity* to be sampled (e.g. 20 magazines), *frequency* (e.g. every fortnight), and *length of time* (e.g. over 6 months).

- **Develop categories** – The researcher will need to analyse the material in a systematic manner. One way to do this is by developing *behavioural categories*. They can be viewed as 'pigeon holes', the researcher analyses the material to find examples (e.g. 'I was not close to my mother') that can be extracted and recorded under the appropriate category. Or they may decide to merely count and record how often instances occur using a tally score (e.g. how many times a negative word is said). Depending on what the researcher wants to investigate, the analysis of the material can be based on words, themes, concepts, images. Below is an example of a content analysis study based on themes.

	Love	War	Poverty	Drugs	Friendships	Family
FEmale	37	5	1	1	6	4
Male	24	9	3	7	1	2

- **Piloting** – It is important when developing the categories that they each have clearly defined operational definitions. They are not vague, but the researchers (coders) need to know exactly what they are recording in each category. A way to assess this is by carrying out a *pilot study*. This allows the researchers a 'test run' to ensure that the coders are trained and agree on classifying the information in the correct category. This can be assessed by having two or more coders independently analysing the material to see whether there is a high agreed consistently (85%+) of categorising data correctly. If so, we can claim that the way the data is recorded by the coders is reliable (inter-rater reliability), which helps reduce researcher bias. Once any issue is corrected the researcher can begin analysing and recording the data.

- **Presentation** – Once the material is analysed and recorded into the appropriate categories, this produces quantitative data that can now be counted (e.g. tally scores). Then it can be presented visually using bar-charts, tables, averages and percentages. A written summary is included, enabling the researcher to draw conclusions from the findings.

Thematic analysis

One way to summarise qualitative material is through the use of **thematic analysis**. This involves a qualitative analysis where the information is summarised and presented in written form, instead of being reduced into numerical form as in content analysis. So, for example, to examine questionnaires or interview transcripts, the process may involve:

- **Development of categories** – The researcher will extract and group information such as examples of sentences, phrases, words and quotations together that are similar, and place them under common themes (categories). The researcher may construct the different types of categories before they examine the data based on the research purpose (known as *pre-existing categories*). Alternatively the categories are created after the researcher examines the data in order to discover any emerging repeating themes they may not have identified initially (known as *emergent categories*).

- **Presentation** – The themes may be grouped together under certain headings and 'subheadings' and discussed, supported by the use of examples and quotations and arriving at some conclusions from the findings.

✓✗ Evaluation

> **✓ Conclusions can be drawn.**
> Content/thematic analysis is a very useful research technique for analysing and summarising a large body of qualitative material, allowing the researcher to draw a conclusion from the data.

> **✓ No researcher effect.**
> Content/thematic analysis does not involve the researcher interacting with the participants because the information has already been gathered. This means that the research cannot influence the participants' behaviour, which makes the results more valid.

> **✓ Reliable.**
> The data produced from content/thematic analysis is reliable. This is because it can easily be repeated by other researchers using the same content analysis frame to see whether the same results are found.

> **✗ Loss of insight.**
> Content analysis means counting up numbers and then describing the pattern or relationship that these numbers seem to suggest. This can be of limited use as it cannot offer explanations as to why such patterns and relationships occur in the first place.

> **✗ Reliability and validity issues.**
> Content/thematic analysis relies on the researcher's subjective interpretation. Different researchers may have different interpretations of the material, which may result in the recorded data being placed in incorrect categories. This inconsistency reduces the reliability and validity of the findings.

> **✗ Unrepresentative.**
> A weakness of content/thematic analysis is that the few selected sample materials may be unrepresentative (e.g. the selection of a few books or an interview transcript), which makes the findings difficult to generalise from.

Summary of the type of data research methods

Quantitative data	Qualitative data
· Experiments	· Unstructured observations
· Controlled observations	· Unstructured interviews
· Structured interviews	· Open-ended questionnaires
· Close-ended questionnaires	· Case studies

Comparing quantitative data and qualitative data

You will realise that the strength of one type is the weakness of the other (and vice versa!)

	Good	Bad
Quantitative data	**Easy to analyse** – summarising numbers makes it easy to analyse the relationship and draw conclusions from the data	**Low in validity** – reducing thoughts and feelings to numbers limits a deeper understanding of human behaviour and experiences
Qualitative data	**High in validity** – as it provides a detailed account into human behaviour and experiences	**Difficult to analyse** – makes drawing a conclusion difficult

Exam Questions

1. Explain what is meant by the term 'content analysis'. . . . . **(2 marks)**

2. Explain one strength and one weakness of content analysis. . . . . **(2+2 marks)**

3. Explain the difference between quantitative and qualitative data. . . . . **(2 marks)**

4. Explain one strength and one weakness of qualitative data. . . . . **(2+2 marks)**

5. Explain one strength and one weakness of quantitative data.. . . . . **(2+2 marks)**

6. In an observational study, 100 cars were fitted with video cameras to record the drivers' behaviour. Two psychologists used content analysis to analyse the data from the films. They found that 75% of accidents involved a lack of attention by the driver. The most common distractions were using a hands-free phone or talking to a passenger. Other distractions included looking at the scenery, smoking, eating, personal grooming and trying to reach something within the car. Explain how the psychologists might have carried out content analysis to analyse the film clips of driver behaviour. . . . . **(4 marks)**

The AQA specification:

A-LEVEL ONLY

- Case studies

The exam requires that you are able to:

▶ Describe, identify and apply your knowledge of case studies.
▶ Give one advantage and two weaknesses associated with case studies.

Introduction

A **case study** is a research method that involves studying an individual or a small group of individuals. They enable the researcher to gather a detailed and descriptive account of those being studied.

Case studies

There is no single way to conduct a case study but they often involve a combination of methods such as observations, interviews, and psychological tests to build up a rich and detailed case history of an individual.

For example, Koluchová (1972) used a case study to investigate the Czech twin boys and Curtiss (1977) made a case study of Genie. Both examined in great depth the extreme case of children who are brought up in isolation, with minimal human contact (see page 53–54).

How case studies help us
- They help us to explore and describe human behaviour in much greater depth.
- They provide a detailed description of a rare or unusual phenomenon.
- They generate theories or hypotheses that can be further explored through other more controlled research methods.
- They challenge existing theories or studies on human behaviour.

✓✗ Evaluation

✓ **Rich qualitative data.**
Case studies allow the researcher to provide rich and detailed information and insight and understanding of human behaviour, more so than any other research methods, such as experiments. This is especially true when the use of experiments would be impractical or unethical to use.

✓ **Contradicts established theories.**
Case studies can be used to test or contradict existing psychological theories. For example, the case study of the severely deprived Czech twins showed that they made a strong recovery when placed in a caring social environment, which challenged Bowlby's established hypothesis on maternal deprivation (whereby the lack of attachment can irreversibly damage a child's social and cognitive development).

✗ **Generalisation is an issue.**
The findings from each case study are difficult to generalise. This is because each case study is based on a single individual whose experience has been unusual and unique. So whatever was discovered to be true of that one case, we cannot guarantee it will be true of other similar cases.

✗ **Observer bias.**
Case studies are prone to observer bias because of the high level of interaction of the researcher with the participant. This can lead to the researcher developing a close relationship with the participants, and may lead to the researcher to become biased in the interpretation and use of data that will affect the outcome of the results.

✗ **Unable to establish a causal relationship.**
Case studies are carried out in an open environment where variables cannot be controlled, and which may influence the findings. This means that case studies are unable to establish a cause-and-effect relationship between the variables.

✗ **Memory distortion.**
Case studies often rely on the person's recollections of past events, and these are prone to omission and distortion. The person may leave out or distort important details during the investigation (intentionally or unintentionally) when the information is collected retrospectively.

Exam Questions

1. Explain what is meant by the term 'case study'.. . . . . **(2 marks)**
2. Give one advantage of using case studies.. . . . . **(2 marks)**
3. Give two weaknesses of using case studies. **(2+2 marks)**

The AQA specification:

- Aims: stating aims, the difference between aims and hypotheses.
- Hypotheses: directional and non-directional.

The exam requires that you are able to:

▶ Describe, identify and formulate an aim.
▶ Describe, identify and formulate a hypothesis (directional and non-directional).
▶ Describe, identify and formulate an independent and a dependent variable.

Aims

All psychology research investigations start off with an **aim.** An aim is a **general statement** that describes the purpose of the study, so people have a general idea of what the research is about (often has the word 'investigate', 'examine', or 'aim' in the sentence). So, for example, an aim could be:

To investigate the influence of sugary soft drinks on memory recall

Hypothesis

Once you know the general aim of your research project, this will now need to be narrowed down further to formulate a **research hypothesis.** A hypothesis is a specific and precise *testable* statement that involves making a *prediction* (not a question) between the two variables or more that the researcher wants to investigate. An example of a hypothesis is:

Participants who drink one pint of sugary drink will do better in a recall word test than those who do not drink a pint of sugary drink.

Types of hypothesis

- **Experimental hypothesis** – The hypothesis is called an experimental hypothesis (H1) when the study is using an *experimental method*.

- **Alternative hypothesis** – In all other *non-experimental research* (e.g. questionnaires, interviews and observations) it is called an alternative hypothesis (Ha). However, the alternative hypothesis is generally used to refer to all types of research methods, whether experimental or non-experimental.

- **Null hypothesis** – The null hypothesis (Ho) is a statement of prediction that the results will *show no relationship* or *no difference* between the variables. The word 'null' means *non-existent*.

Null hypothesis

Psychologists must initially assume when carrying out an investigation that there is no relationship or difference between the variables (e.g. sugary drinks and memory recall). It is the job of the alternative hypothesis to prove that there is a relationship and thus prove that the null hypothesis is wrong! Therefore in a research study there are really *two* hypotheses that are being investigated, the null hypothesis and the alternative hypothesis (as an alternative to the null hypothesis). Here is an example of a null hypothesis:

There will be no difference in a recall word test between participants who drink one pint of sugary drink from those who did not consume a sugary drink.

How do we prove which hypothesis is right?

If we found that the results of the memory recall test showed a *very small* difference between people who consumed sugary drinks and those who did not, we would say that the results are not significant enough, because a small difference was probably due to a chance factor, and not due to the sugary drink itself, but due to something else, like tiredness. This means we would have to accept the null hypothesis – that sugary drinks (the IV) does not have an effect on memory recall (the DV).

However, if the results showed a *large* difference between the groups, we could say that the results are significant enough that the difference could *not* have been down to chance alone, but must be due to the sugary drink (the IV). We would have to accept the alternative hypothesis – that the sugary drink (the IV) had an effect on memory recall (the DV).

Directional and non-directional hypotheses

A hypothesis can either be:

- **A directional (one-tailed) hypothesis** – This predicts that there will be a difference in the results and the *direction* the results will go in. An example of a directional hypothesis: 'Boys are more aggressive than girls during adolescence.' This tells us there is a difference (i.e. between boys and girls) and direction of the results (i.e. boys are more aggressive than girls).

- **Non-directional (two-tailed) hypothesis** – This does not predict the direction the results will go in—they can go either way. For example, a non-directional hypothesis for the aggression study will be: 'There is a difference in aggressive behaviour between boys and girls during adolescence.' The hypothesis predicts that there is a difference in aggressive behaviour between the genders, but does not predict whether boys or girls are *more* aggressive. Thus the hypothesis is *not* directed towards either boys or girls and thus, it is a non-directional hypothesis.

Which one do you choose – directional and non-directional hypotheses?

Some researchers use a *directional* hypothesis because similar research carried out before has produced results that have gone in a particular direction. A *non-directional* hypothesis may be used when similar research previously carried out has produced unclear or contradictory results, so the researcher is not sure what the outcome will be.

Operationalisation of variables

Once the hypothesis has been established, the researcher needs to put the variables into *operational definitions* – this is **operationalisation**. It is the process of converting the variables in a way that can be tested and measured in practical terms (i.e. *how* will you go about doing that?) This means that the researcher will need to define exactly *how* the independent variable will be tested, and *how* the dependent variable will be measured.

Look at the following two example hypotheses:

> **Watching violent videos leads to physically aggressive behaviour in young children.**
> Violent video (the IV) can be operationalised by exposure to set of three violent twenty minute children's cartoon, one after the other. Aggressive behaviour (the DV) could be measured by the number of 'kicks' or 'punches' the child carries out during playtime at school.

Middle-class children are less likely to experience stress than working-class children.
Social class (the IV) can be operationalised by using questionnaires to assess details of the parental occupation, income and housing, and so on, as an indicator of the children's social class. Stress (the DV) could be assessed by a questionnaire using a scoring system.

Why operationalisation of variables is so important
Clear operational definitions are important so that researchers can replicate a study in exactly the same manner as the original so they can compare the results, and thus assess the reliability and validity of the original study.

Exam Questions

1. A psychologist carried out an experiment to see whether the older you become the less you are able to recall information correctly from short-term memory. In the young group, participants were aged between 15 and 40 years and in the elderly group, they were aged between 75 and 90 years. The two groups of participants were presented with a list of words of everyday shopping items and were asked to recall the words immediately in the correct order.

   a) Write a suitable aim for this study. . . . . **(2 marks)**

   b) Write a suitable non-directional hypothesis for this study. . . . . **(2 marks)**

   c) Explain what is meant by the term 'operationalisation'. . . . . **(2 marks)**

The AQA specification:

- Sampling: the difference between population and sample; sampling techniques including: random, systematic, stratified, opportunity and volunteer; implications of sampling techniques, including bias and generalisation.

The exam requires that you are able to:

▶ Identify, describe and apply your knowledge of the different sampling techniques.
▶ Explain how the sampling techniques can lead to bias and affect the generalisability of the findings.

Key terms

- **Target population.** The large group of people that the psychologist is interested in researching in order to draw conclusions about their views or behaviour. (E.g. mothers, teenagers, children, or more specifically all single mothers, teenagers from 16-18 years of age or all children under 4 years of age.)

- **Sampling frame.** A sampling frame is a list of all names included in the target population from which the sample will be drawn, such as telephone books, registers of electors, school rolls or lists of patients.

- **Sample.** The process of selecting a small group of participants from the sampling frame to take part in the study.

- **Generalisability.** How much the sample 'represents' (is representative of) the larger population, in that conclusions from the research on the sample can be 'generalised' to the wider population.

- **Biased sample.** A sample that does not represent the target population.

Introduction

Part of the research process is finding participants to take part in a study. It would be impossible for a researcher to carry out a study on the entire target population as it would be impractical, time consuming and expensive. So a small selection of participants is chosen to take part in the study—this is known as a sample.

The aim of a sample is to allow the findings collected from a study to be *representative* (i.e. typical) of the target population. This means it is possible for the researcher to be able to make valid *generalisations* or *conclusions* about the larger group that were *not* included in the study. So for example, if the psychologist is interested in the reliability of eye-witness testimonies of very young children, they would ideally want the theory to explain the reliability of eye-witness testimony of all such children, not just the ones in the study.

Sampling techniques

There are different sampling techniques that the researcher can use to maximise the generalisability of the findings. However, each technique has its weaknesses which can lead to having a biased sample which will affect the generalisability of the findings, as the sample is not reflective of the general population. This means the study has low ecological validity. The sampling techniques covered are:

Random Sampling	Systematic sampling	Stratified sampling	Opportunity sampling	Volunteer sampling

Random sampling

Random sampling means *every* person in the target population has an equal chance of being randomly selected for the sample. Random sampling is a way to remove bias in sample selection. The sample can be selected by:

- **Manual selection.** If the population size is small (e.g. students from a local sixth-form college) the names could be written on pieces of paper, placed in a box or hat, shuffled (after each draw) and then the names picked out until the required sample size is reached.
- **Random number generator.** For a larger population, a computer program (random number generator) can be used to generate a list of random numbers, which are then matched up with the names (and addresses) to produce the required sample size.

✗ Generalisability and bias

✗ Can lead to a biased sample.
With random sampling, there is still a small possibility that you could end up with a biased sample of people (too many females, males, certain social class, occupation, age and so on). In terms of age, you may end up with too many students in the sample compared to non-students (e.g. working adults). This will make the sample unrepresentative of the target population that you are studying and therefore it will be hard to make generalisations from the research findings.

✗ May refuse to take part or drop out.
There is also the real possibility that one or more people selected may not wish to take part in the study, or are hard to get hold of, or they may just drop out. This can lead to a reduced sample, or the researcher may choose another random participant, which by the very fact that they were not originally 'randomly chosen' can result in having a biased sample.

✗ Costly and time consuming.
When the target population is very large, it is simply too costly and time consuming to gather all the names on a database of people from all over the country. Therefore the researcher will resort to creating his own sampling frame list from a particular place (e.g. university, city) and draw the sample from a local name directory/register. This means that not every one is equally likely to be chosen and so the sample is not truly random; instead, it is biased towards 'people on your list'. For example, they may be drawn from a particular area and could be an over-representation of either a wealthy, poor or particular ethnic group.

✗ Electoral register/directories not representative.
The existing directories or registers may not have all the members of the population on the list. For example, if we take an electoral register, this excludes those not old enough to vote and those who indicated that they do not wish to vote in elections. Also certain social or ethnic groups, such as the poor, may be under-represented on the electoral register because they may not have registered to vote.

Systematic sampling

Systematic sampling is when the sample is predetermined by choosing every nth name from the sampling frame, such as selecting every fourth person in a school list of all the students. For example, if we want a 10% sample from 800 students you may choose a random number, such as every tenth person, from the sampling frame until you get the desired amount required (i.e. 80 students).

✗ Generalisability and bias

✗ Can lead to a biased sample.
Systematic sampling is not totally random, since not everyone has an equal chance of being chosen. This is because the sample is drawn from a sample frame in a systematic way; this can bias the results, and thus will not be an accurate representation of the target population. For example, every tenth name might, purely by chance, happen to be a white middle-class person. For a more elaborate explanation, imagine a city where exactly half the population is male and half female. Suppose we take a 1% sample, (one person in every hundred). This will give us a sample of 1000 people. Yet by chance it could happen that our sample contains, say, 600 females and 400 males, rather than 500 of each gender.

Opportunity sampling

Opportunity sampling (convenience sampling) is when researchers themselves approach anyone who is easily available or accessible and willing to participate. This is probably the easiest way to acquire participants and it is often chosen for this practical reason. It can be done by asking passers-by in the street or in a shopping mall, for example, whether they are available and willing to take part in a research study. Typically researchers who are based in psychology departments ask their psychology students to take part in a study.

✗ Generalisability and bias

✗ Can lead to a biased sample.
The people selected using opportunity sampling could lead to the researcher having a biased sample. The researcher would have selected the people who were available at that time and willing to take part. This means the people available at that time may be of a particular social group. For example, asking people mid-week during the day will result in a higher percentage of mothers, students or those who are not working. This makes it is hard to make generalisations from the research findings because the people are chosen are from a narrow population and not representative of the target population (wider population).

✗ Students are not representative.
Using university students could lead to a biased sample because students are not representative of the population as a whole. University students tend to be young, middle-class, more literate and intelligent than the general population. This reduces the generalisability of the findings, as the sample is not reflective of the wider population. This means the study will have low ecological validity.

Volunteer sampling

Volunteer sampling (or self-selecting sampling) is when participants have freely chosen to be part of the study by responding to an advertisement in newspapers, leaflets, television, radio or by word of mouth.

✗ Generalisability and bias

✗ Can lead to a biased sample.
Volunteer sampling is prone to bias. This is because participants who opt to take part often have certain social or personal characteristics that are different from those who donot volunteer. They may be more educated, more enthusiastic, motivated, social or obedient; none of which may be typical of the general population. This can make the sample unrepresentative and therefore it will be hard to make generalisations from the research findings.

Stratified sampling

One way to overcome the probability that the sample of people selected is not very representative (such as those chosen by random sampling and systematic sampling) is to reduce the sampling bias by using stratified random sampling. The sampling frame is divided into strata (sub-categories) and then a certain number of people are randomly selected from each of these sub-categories in proportion to its representation in the target population. These can be any characteristics or variables that the researcher is interested in, such as gender, age, class and ethnicity. For example, if we wanted to carry out a survey on Year 12 and Year 13 students to see if there is a gender difference in their views on the legalisation of cannabis, we could 'stratify' the sampling frame into four separate categories, e.g. Year 12 boys; Year 12 girls; Year 13 boys and Year 13 girls. If want a 10% representative sample, we can then select the amount of students from each category in proportion to its numbers. So if there are only 50 Year 12 boy students, then five (10%) will be chosen randomly to be part of the sample.

Sampling and research methods

Research method (commonly used)	Sampling technique (commonly used)
Laboratory experiments	Opportunity sampling, volunteer sampling
Field experiments	Opportunity sampling
Self-report (questionnaires/interviews)	Random sampling, volunteer sampling, opportunity sampling
Observational research	Time sampling, event sampling

Exam Questions

1. A researcher is interested in studying the experiences of twins raised together and comparing them to twins raised apart. They obtain a register of all the twins in the UK. The researcher chooses all those in the register whose last name begins with H or Z because there are so many names that start with H or B. The researcher then randomly selects a sample of 20 twins from this list.

   a) The psychologist used a random sampling method. Explain how he could have obtained his sample using this method. . . . . **(3 marks)**

   b) Explain the limitations of using random sampling in this study. . . . . **(3 marks)**

2. A boys' secondary school has agreed to let a researcher conduct a student survey on bullying. The researcher obtains the school's electronic register with the names of all the students between 11 and 18 years of age. The researcher has decided to select 100 students to answer his questionnaire and is interested in getting a range of views from all year groups.

   a) Suggest one sample method that could provide a range of views. . . . . **(1 mark)**

   b) Explain how the researcher could obtain a sample using this method. . . . . **(3 marks)**

3. Every January large numbers of people join a gym to get fit, but then stop going after a few months. A team of psychologists decided to investigate why this happens. The psychologists contacted several gyms and asked permission to interview those people who joined during January. They put up posters in each of the gyms, asking for people to take part in their study.

   a) Identify the sampling method used to select participants in this study. Justify your answer.. . . **(2 marks)**

   b) Explain one limitation of the sampling method used to select participants for this study. . . . **(3 marks)**

The AQA specification: Research Methods

Investigation design

- Pilot studies

The exam requires that you are able to:

▶ Describe the purpose of a pilot study.

Introduction

Whatever type of research method is chosen, a **pilot study** is often carried out. This is a technique whereby the researcher carries out a small-scale practice run on a few participants before the real research begins.

Purpose of pilot studies

The purpose of a pilot study is to reveal any design problems relating to questions, material, procedures, instructions, data handling, and so on, in the research study. It saves a lot of time and money by identifying early on any design flaws, so that they can be amended before the 'real thing' begins. Naturally this helps to *improve the reliability* and *validity* of the design.

Experiments

In experiments, participants can give feedback on the *procedures*. For example, the researcher might want to know whether the instructions were easily understood or were they confusing to the participants? Was the *experimental task* appropriate? Was there enough time to complete it? Does it need less or more time? Did the participants guess the hypothesis of the investigation? If so, the researcher may need to think about redesigning the experimental task (which will help the researcher reduce the demand characteristics).

Self-report methods

For self-report methods (questionnaires and interviews), a pilot study could be used to evaluate the construction of the questions, to see whether they are difficult or confusing, relevant to the aims of the study, and all understood in the same way by all the respondents. As a result, some questions will be amended or omitted.

Controlled observational research

In controlled observational research, a pilot study helps identify any potential problems with the design of the behavioural checklist. It allows the opportunity to see whether two or more researchers are consistent in the way they record information, that is, the behaviour being observed is interpreted and categorised in the same way (and not differently).

Exam Questions

1. Explain what is meant by the term 'pilot study'.. . . . . **(2 marks)**

2. Explain one reason why a pilot study should be carried out in psychological research when using self-report techniques.. . . . . **(3 marks)**

The AQA specification:

- Control of extraneous variables
- Demand characteristics and investigator effects

The exam requires that you are able to:

▶ Identify what extraneous variables, demand characteristics and investigator effects are, describe them and suggest ways of controlling them.

Introduction

Extraneous variables, demand characteristics and investigator effects are all unwanted variables (factors) that can threaten the validity of a study. Part of the design process for the researcher is to identify and **control** or **reduce** them as far as possible.

Extraneous variables in experimental research

Extraneous variables (EV) can be defined as anything other than the independent variable (IV) that could affect the dependent variable (DV). One of the reasons why laboratory experiments are viewed as the most scientific method is their high level of control over EV. If such variables are not controlled, or at least minimised, they can confound the results, which will threaten the validity of a study. There two main types of EV – participant variables and situational variables.

EV: Participant variables

Participant variables can be viewed as differences in the characteristics and behaviours of the participants, which can influence the experiment and thus act as an EV.

- **Individual differences:** Individual differences and behaviours of the participants themselves can influence the results of the experiment (e.g. age, intelligence, gender, ethnicity, social class, experience, skills, tiredness, mood and motivation). This is only an issue if the experimental design is an *independent group design*.

Ways to control participant variables

- **Randomisation (random assignment)**

One way to control individual differences is to use randomisation in independent group design. The use of random assignment means that each participant has an equal chance of being assigned 'randomly' to any of the two conditions in the experiment. The idea is that any unequal characteristics in their age, IQ or personality, for instance, will be evenly distributed across the groups, thus controlling the unwanted variables. Randomisation makes it less likely that one group will have more unwanted variables than the other group.

- **Repeated measures**

Another way to control individual differences is to use repeated measures design when it is appropriate.

EV: Situational variables
Situational variables relate to any features of the experiment, that may affect the participant's behaviour and thus act as an EV.

- **Environmental factors:** These relate to the features of the experiment, that may affect the participant's behaviour, such as the instructions given, the material used, noise, temperature, lighting, the time of day and so on.

- **Demand characteristics:** Participants naturally want to guess want the study is about. Any features of the experiment (e.g. tasks, equipment, video clips) may act as a clue. Participants will (consciously or unconsciously) change their behaviour in a way that they think the study 'demands' it. Demand characteristics can affect the validity of the findings, because the participant does not behave as they normally would.

- **Investigator effects:** The investigator can influence the behaviour of the participants. This may be due to the investigator's social and personal characteristics (age, gender, class, ethnicity, attractiveness, mannerism, friendliness, intimidating etc.) or through **investigator expectancy.** This means that the investigator may act in a way that will influence the participants responses towards a desired outcome the researcher wants *(see page 109 for more detail on investigator effects)*.

- **Order effect:** If a repeated measures design is used in an experiment, there is the possibility of order effect and demand characteristics. There are two types of order effect. With the **practice effect**, any improvement in performance in the second condition might be due to participants already had a practice at doing the task in the first condition. Equally, if performance is worsened through doing the experiment twice, this might be due to boredom, which is known as the **fatigue effect**. Either way, this would be counted as a confounding variable.

Ways to control situational variables

- **Standardisation of instructions and procedures**
One way to *control environmental factors* is to ensure that the procedures and instructions in the experiment given to the participants are *standardised.* This means all the participants are instructed in the same way and tested under the same conditions.

- **Single-blind procedure**
One way to *control demand characteristics* is to use a *single-blind procedure*. This is when participants do not know the true aim of the experiment (i.e. deception is used), and/or are told something entirely different.

- **Double-blind procedure**
One way to *control investigator effect* and *demand characteristics* is to use the *double-blind procedure*. This is when the investigator and the participants are both kept in the dark about the true aim of the experiment.

- **Counterbalancing**
One way to *control order effect* and *demand chrematistics* in *repeated measures design* is to use counterbalancing *(see Exam Notes 2).*

Extraneous variables:
Demand characteristics and investigator effects in all research methods
EVs such as *demand characteristics* and *investigator effect* are not solely the problem of experimental research – they can occur in all types of research methods used (e.g. interviews and observations).

EV: Demand characteristics

Demand characteristics refers to the **research situation** in which participants finds themselves, which can influence how the participant behave. Demand characteristics can act as an EV because the participant does not behave as they normally would. Below are some different types of demand characteristics:

- **Guessing what the study is about** – Participants naturally will be curious and try to guess want the study is about. The participants unconsciously seek clues from any features (characteristics) of the research situation such as the instructions given, the type of tasks or tests performed or questions asked. Participants may then change their behaviour if they think the study 'demands' a particular response – to what they think is expected of them, hence the term 'demand characteristics'. If this is the case, all the participants are likely to behave in the same type of way because the research situation may have 'invited' (unknowingly) a particular response.

- **Participant effects** (or **participant reactivity**) – Some participants in a study may affect the validity of the findings because of their own expectation and attitude. The fact that participants are being observed or evaluated may lead them to not behave as they naturally would. Some types of participant effects are:

  - **Social desirability bias** – Participants may attempt to present themselves in a positive light, attempting to make a good impression (more 'desirable'). For example, in an interview or questionnaire they may answer in a way that makes them appear more approving towards the researcher but does not truly reflect their opinion or behaviour. Equally, participants may not be helpful towards the investigation (to annoy the researcher or out of frustration) and may deliberately give a wrong answer or behave differently. This is known as **screw-you-effect**.

  - **Hawthorne effect** – Participants may act differently from how they would do normally, just because of the *attention* they are receiving from the researcher and not because of the manipulation of IV.

Ways to control demand characteristics
- Standardisation of instructions and procedures.
- Single blind procedure.

EV: Investigator effects

The investigator effects is when the investigator behaviour and characteristics influences the behaviour of the participants and thus acts as an EV on the study. There are two main types of the investigator 's effect – *investigator 's characteristics* and *investigator expectancy*.

- **Investigator characteristics** – The physiological and psychological qualities of the investigator, such as age, gender, class, ethnicity and personality type (e.g. friendliness, intimidation) can influence participant behaviour.

- **Investigator expectancy** – The investigator has specific expectations about the outcome of the study, and may unintentionally or intentionally behave (e.g. mannerisms, body language, the use of leading questions) in a way that influences the participants responses, which may in turn produce the outcome the researcher desired from the study.

Ways to control investigator effects
- Double-blind procedures.
- Standardisation of instructions and procedures.

Exam Questions

1. Some psychology students wanted to investigate whether people are more likely to recall more happy words than sad words. Forty students took part in the experiment and a repeated measures design was used. The participants were shown a list of happy words, which they then had to recall. Then they were then shown a list of sad words, which they had to recall.

   a) Suggest one possible extraneous variable in this experiment. **(1 mark)**

   b) Suggest one way the researcher can deal with this extraneous variable. . . . . **(2 marks)**

2. Explain what is meant by the term 'demand characteristics'. . . . . **(2 marks)**

3. Explain what is meant by the term 'investigator effects'. . . . . **(2 marks)**

The AQA specification:

- Ethics, including the role of the British Psychological Society's code of ethics; ethical issues in the design and conduct of psychological studies; dealing with ethical issues in research.

The exam requires that you are able to:

▶ Familiarise yourself with the Code of Ethics.
▶ Describe and identify ethical issues and ways in which psychologists deal with them when they arise.

British Psychological Society (BPS) Code of Ethics

It is important when considering the design of research to ensure that researchers follow the **Code of Ethics and Conduct** published by the **British Psychological Society** (**BPS**). This publication sets out a number of ethical guidelines for psychological researchers to follow when carrying out research on people (and animals). It aims to ensure that organisations, such as universities and hospitals, that carry out research studies follow certain ethical guidelines. To ensure that they do, these organisations have their own internal **ethics committees**.

The role of these committees is to assess and advise on ethical matters or issues arising for the researchers within their organisation who wish to carry out a study. Any researchers who break the guidelines may have their licence withdrawn from the BPS, which means that they can no longer practise as a psychologist.

Content of the BPS Code of Ethics

Below are the main themes covered in the BPS guidelines for ethics and conduct. The publication is regularly updated and revised.

Consent

Before agreeing to take part in a study, the participants will need to be fully informed about the purpose of the study. This includes the researcher explaining the aims and procedure and how the data will be used in the study. They will also be informed about their rights – that no harm will come to them, that they can withdraw from the investigation at any time (even if money was given to them for taking part) and that their confidentiality and anonymity will be respected. Only after being fully informed, can the participant give written consent. Children under the age of 16 years need the consent of a parent or guardian.

Deception

The use of deception in a study means that the participants are deliberately misled or lied to, or that vital information was withheld about the true purpose of the study. The BPS states that investigators should try to avoid using deception where possible.

Debriefing

Once the study has ended, the investigator will need to debrief the participants. This involves fully informing them about the purpose of the study – especially if deception was used (and justifying why it was necessary) – and reminding them that the information will be kept confidential and their right to withdraw their data at any time. Debriefing also gives the participants an opportunity to have a conversation and ask questions about the study, thus making sure that they were unaffected by taking part (and came to no psychological harm).

Right to withdraw

Right from the beginning, when informed consent is given, it should also be made clear to participants that they have the right to withdraw from the study. This means they can leave at any time – regardless of whether a payment was given or some other form of inducement was offered. Participants are also made aware that they have the right to withdraw any data they have provided, and that it can be destroyed, even when the study has been completed and the data has been collected.

Confidentiality

Participants are guaranteed that all information collected from them during the study will be kept private – unless there are legal, safety or health obligations. Anonymity is part of confidentiality. If, for example, the study is published, letters, numbers or pseudonym names should be given instead of the participants' real names, so that the information cannot be identifiable as theirs.

Protection of participants

Researchers have the responsibility to protect participants from any physical and psychological harm (e.g. being anxious, distressed, having feelings of low-esteem or embarrassment) during the investigation. Normally, the risk of harm must be no greater than in ordinary life. This means that participants should not be exposed to risks greater than (or additional to) those encountered during their normal lifestyles.

Observational research

Studies based on observation must respect the privacy and psychological well-being of the individuals during a research investigation. Unless those being observed give their consent to being observed, observational research is *only* acceptable in situations where the observed people would *expect* to be observed by strangers in a normal everyday environment (like waiting in a bus queue or being served in a restaurant).

How psychologists deal with ethical issues

Even with ethical guidelines like these in place, there are times when carrying out a study may conflict with the rights of the participants. For example, the researcher may need to consider lying to the participants about the real purpose of the study (which is deception). Sometimes there is the possibility of causing distress to participants. Ethical issues may arise when designing a research project, and the researcher will need deal with these. The three main ethical issues that often arise in psychological research are obtaining consent, the use of deception and protection of the participants. How psychologists deal with each of these is described in the table below.

Informed consent

The issues

- The participants may have consented to take part, although they may not have been fully informed about the true purpose of the study. This means deception has been used. Deception is sometimes necessary, because explaining the true aims of the study sometimes affects the participants' behaviour (demand characteristics) and thus reduces the validity of the research.

- In field studies (e.g. observational research and field experiments) the participants are unaware that they are being investigated. Therefore, informed consent is difficult or impossible to obtain.

- Young children or people with disabilities or impairments may have limited understanding and therefore they may not fully understand much about the research investigation – even if they have given informed consent.

Informed consent

How to deal with these issues

- **Presumptive consent** involves asking members of the general population who are similar to the participants in the study whether they would consider the research procedures to be acceptable and whether they would be willing to participate in such an investigation.

- **Prior general consent** involves telling those who volunteer to take part in the research study that they *may* be deceived about the true nature of the study. Only those who agree with this are selected. In this way, they have given general informed consent, but they do not know the real aims of the study. This is also known as **partially informed consent**.

- In studies involving children under 16, consent is obtained from the parents or from those *in loco parentis*, which means 'in the place of a parent' (e.g. a carer or a headteacher in a school).

- For participants who have impairments that limit their understanding, the investigator should consult a person well-placed to appreciate their reactions, such as a member of their family.

Deception

The issues

- Deception means lying to the participants – which is wrong. However some argue that the use of deception is unavoidable at times, and needs to be used to avoid the participants changing their normal behaviour (e.g. demand characteristics).

- If participants have been deceived, they could not have been fully informed and therefore were unable to consent because they did not know the true purpose of the study.

How to deal with these issues

- If deception has taken place, participants should be **debriefed** at the end of the research study. This means that they should be fully informed about the true purpose of the investigation and told the reason for the deception. They are also reminded that the information will be kept confidential and that they have the right to withdraw their data from the study if they wish.

- In general, the aim of debriefing is to restore the participant to the state he or she was in at the start of the investigation.

Protection of participants

The issues

- Some studies require that the participants experience some form of physical harm, such as putting their hands into very cold water. The research cannot always fully predict the amount of harm that this may cause to the participants. Psychological harm may also be caused; however, this is more difficult to measure. It may arise if participants are made to experience undesirable feelings (such as embarrassment), especially if other people are involved and/or watching.

- Probing questionnaires or interviews that involve revealing personal information run the risk of provoking negative feelings (such as lowered esteem and worthlessness) and these may have long-term effects.

How to deal with these issues

- **The right to withdraw** – Participants who consented to take part in the study should also be made aware that they have right to withdraw from the research at any point, regardless of any payment received, if they become uncomfortable with it. The data gathered about them will then be removed and destroyed.

- **Stopping the research** – The researcher should look out for any physical or psychological signs (e.g. negative feelings) and stop any situation that may cause harm to a participant. If they see this occurring with a number of participants, they should stop the entire study to prevent any lasting harm to the participants.

- **Participant information** – Participants must be asked about any factors that might pose a risk, such as pre-existing medical conditions, and must be advised of any special action they should take to avoid risk.

Main ethical issues affecting different research methods

RESEARCH METHODS	MAIN ETHICAL ISSUE
Laboratory experiments	• **Deception –** Participants may not know the true purpose of the study (reduce demand characteristics) in order to preserve the validity of the study. • **Informed consent –** May not be possible for the participant to be fully informed about the true purpose of the study when deception is used.
Field and natural experiments	• **Informed consent –** Consent is very unlikely to be obtained if participants are not aware they are taking part in a study. • **Right to withdraw –** Participants should have the right to withdraw from a study at any time. If they do not know they are part of a study, they will not know about this right!
Correlational analysis	• **Problem of interpretation –** Published research findings may reveal socially sensitive information (e.g. regarding ethnicity and crime) which could be misinterpreted by the public as a cause-and-effect relationship.
Observations	• **Informed consent –** Consent is very unlikely to be obtained if participants are not aware they are taking part in a study. • **Invasion of privacy –** If participants are not aware they are being observed (especially if observing in non-public setting such as a school), this raises the issues of invasion of privacy.
Questionnaires and interviews	• **Confidentiality –** Questions can reveal personal beliefs, opinion and attitudes. Confidentiality can be an issue if this cannot be guaranteed by the researcher. The participant must be told in advance if this is the case.
Case studies	• **Invasion of privacy –** The researcher needs to ensure confidentiality. If this cannot be guaranteed, the participant must be told in advance.

Exam Questions

1. A psychologist wants to investigate the effects of day-care on the behaviour of young children. He decides to observe a class of children at a day-care centre.

    a) Identify one ethical issue the psychologist will need to consider . . . . **(1 mark)**

    b) Explain how the researcher could deal with this ethical issue. . . . . **(3 marks)**

2. Some psychological research requires the use of deception.
    Explain one possible way the psychologist may deal with the use of deception. . . . . **(3 marks)**

3. Some psychological research requires the recall of painful memories, such as being a witness to a violent criminal act. A possible ethical issue that might arise during this research is the protection of participants from harm. Explain one possible way in which the psychologist may deal with this ethical issue. . . . . **(3 marks)**

The AQA specification:

- Validating new knowledge and the role of peer review

The exam requires that you are able to:

▶ Understand and describe the role of peer review in validating new knowledge.

Key terms

- **Peer review (also called 'refereeing').** A Peer review is a process whereby a scientist submits their research paper prior to publication, to be critically evaluated by other scientists (hence 'peers') who are experts in the area. The aim is to ensure the quality of the piece of research in terms of research design and validity, as well as the contribution to scientific knowledge it makes.

- **Journals.** Scientific journals are like magazine publications which publish new research studies that have been peer reviewed. They may be published weekly, monthly or less frequently. There are thousands of different journals that specialise in the different academic disciplines (psychology, physics ,chemistry, etc.) and the sub-disciplines (e.g. in psychology the *Journal of Personality and Social Psychology, Journal of Cognitive Psychology and Journal of Social Psychology*). Journals are read mostly by practising academic researchers, rather than the general public.

Introduction

Scientific knowledge can only progress if the researchers share their findings with one another and with the general public. Therefore the final step in the scientific investigation is to write up a concise summary of the study and its findings (see Figure 1.1) and submit the research article to a journal for publication. Scientific journals represent the most vital means of disseminating (circulating widely) research findings to the scientific community. When articles are submitted to scientific journals they go through a demanding process known as *peer review,* whereby other scientific experts in the same field critically evaluate the study's design, data analyses and conclusions, as well as its contribution to scientific knowledge and theory. The sharing of research with other academic peers in the scientific community is an important part of this scientific process as it is a form of scientific 'quality control' before new knowledge is validated. The intention of peer reviewing is to ensure that any research conducted and published is of high quality. It is generally agreed that that journal's articles, published after a process of peer review, have greater merit than those published in journals not subject to peer review.

The layout of a psychological research report

The standard format of a research report in a journal consists of the following elements:

Author	Method
Title	Results
Abstract	Discussion
Introduction	References

How the peer review process works

- After a researcher has conducted a study, it will need to be written down as a research paper (article) and then submitted to the editor of the appropriate scientific journal in which the researcher wishes to publish it.

- The editor of the journal then selects two or three researchers, experts in the field covered by the study, who will independently review the research to see if it is worthy of publication in the journal.

- Generally, the editor will remove any personal information about the author, such as his or her name, so the reviewers do not know the identity of the submitting researcher. The submitting researcher will not learn the identity of those doing the peer review either, in order to reduce any form of bias or prejudice.

- The reviewers independently critically assess the quality of the research paper to ensure that the study is methodologically sound (i.e. its design, analysis and interpretation of the data collection and written quality). The reviewers provide feedback to the editor and make a decision whether to:

   1. Immediately accept the research paper for publication (incredibly rare)

   2. Request that the author 'revise and resubmit' the article based on the reviewers' comments

   3. Reject the article (e.g. errors, poor research design or poorly interpreted results).

The editor, using the feedback provided by the reviewers, will decide whether the research should be *accepted* for publication, or if the research article requires *revision* (e.g. poorly written, clarification or further detail required) prior to publication. The researcher then has an opportunity to change or improve the research paper before it is approved for publication. Alternatively the research paper may be *rejected*.

Why peer-review is important in the research process

Peer review is an important part of this scientific process because it provides a way of checking the overall quality of the research, helping to ensure that poorly conducted studies do not make it into the scientific literature. The reviewers will assess the research paper by looking at:

- **Quality of the research.** It is very unlikely that the researcher would have spotted every mistake; by showing it to other academics it increases the probability that weaknesses will be identified and addressed. The reviewers will scrutinise the quality of the research and the way it was reported (language) such as:

   ○ Looking at the design of the study to ensure adequate controls had been used to eliminate as far as possible extraneous variables. To see if potential sources of bias may have entered the research (e.g. the method used to collect data). If there are weaknesses in the design, then the findings and conclusions would lack validity.

   ○ To identify any ethical or sampling issues – whether the sample was small or was based on a small part of the general population (e.g. gender, ethnic or social class).

   ○ To assess that the data has been correctly analysed and accurately reported.

   ○ To assess the interpretation of the findings and the appropriateness of any conclusions drawn from the study.

- **Peer reviewed has higher integrity.** The peer review process is a major strength of a scientific approach because it helps to ensure that any research paper published in a reputable journal will be viewed with high integrity and reduces the likelihood of publishing erroneous findings. This means the study will be taken seriously by other researchers and the public.

- **Replication.** Replication is another way of validating a research study. Studies published in journals allow other researchers to replicate the study to verify that similar results are recorded. It is possible that the researcher has made errors in their study or, in some (rare) cases, may have deliberately falsified the results (i.e. fraud) which may not have been picked up during the peer peer reviewing process. If a study has been replicated by other researchers and the findings are supported, the scientific community will have greater confidence in the results because they are viewed to be valid and reliable.

✗ Evaluation of peer review

✗ Publication bias.
One criticism of the peer review process is that they tend to favour studies that have positive (significant) results, and are therefore more likely to be published in a journal, than those studies with findings that are non-significant. This selective form of publication gives a misrepresented understanding of the topic as it tends to ignore any research with non-significant results.

✗ Bias in peer review.
One of the weaknesses of peer reviewing is that peer reviewers may have their own biases. For example, the reviewers may be prejudiced against studies that contradict their own research or views, and therefore less likely to give an approval for submission for publication (especially if the reviewers are to remain anonymous). Or they may be biased towards publishing studies in support of their own research or views. However, using multiple reviewers is supposed to balance out this form of bias.

✗ Peer review is not fool proof.
There has been debate as to how effective the peer review process really is in detecting errors in academic papers. Whilst the process can pick out any obvious omissions and errors, peer reviewing is less effective in the detection of fraud, plagiarism or errors in the data. If a scientist knowingly and deliberately sets out to plagiarise or falsify data, a team of reviewers may not be able to detect it. However, the ability of scientists to replicate the results of published research is another quality-control mechanism against such fraudulence.

✗ Peer reviewing can be inconsistent.
Peer review has been accused of being an inconsistent process because the comments provided by the independent reviewers can be so different from each other. They can even differ on whether or not the article should be published. This is because the review process is based on the subjective interpretation of the reviewers. The low reliability of peer reviewing and the low level of agreement among reviewers of the same research paper mean that many have questioned the effectiveness and usefulness of peer reviewing.

Exam Questions

1. Outline what is meant by the term 'peer review' in psychological research. . . . . **(2 marks)**

2. A research paper was subjected to peer review before it was published in a journal.
   Explain why peer review is important in psychological research.. . . . . **(5 marks)**

3. Explain two criticisms of peer review in psychological research.. . . . . **(3 marks + 3 marks)**

The AQA specification: A-LEVEL ONLY

- Observational techniques. Types of observation: naturalistic and controlled observation; covert and overt observation; participant and non-participant observation.

The exam requires that you are able to:

▶ Identify, describe and apply your knowledge of the different types of reliability and validity.
▶ Discuss how reliability and validity in research can be assessed and improved upon.

Key terms

- **Reliability.** The ability of a study or test to produce the same results if it were to be repeated.

- **Internal reliability.** How consistent the measuring instrument or study itself is (e.g. tests, questionnaires, behavioural categories, experimental procedure); ensure that questions or items are all measuring the same thing.

- **External reliability.** Refers to the extent to which a study or measuring instrument is consistent over different times.

- **Validity.** Refers to how well a study or test measures what it claims to measure and the extent to which the findings can be generalised beyond the research setting.

- **Internal validity.** The extent to which the actual study or test correctly measures what it claims to measure.

- **External validity.** The extent to which the results can be generalised beyond the research setting, such as to a different setting (e.g. real world), time period (e.g. past/future) or population (e.g. age/culture).

Introduction

An important aspect when designing a study or a test (e.g. experiment, interview, questionnaire, observations) is to consider the 'reliability' and the 'validity' of the study. There are different ways of assessing the reliability and validity as well as how they can be improved.

Reliability

Experimental and non-experimental methods are used to measure and collect data on human behaviour. It is important that the results we find are consistent (i.e. reliable) if repeated. We can assess the reliability of such methods by taking a closer look at the experimental procedures and the measuring instruments used, such as questionnaires, structured interviews, tests (e.g. personality test) and behavioural categories/coding system (in observations). There are three types of reliability we can use to assess the methods: *Internal reliability, external reliability* and *researcher reliability.*

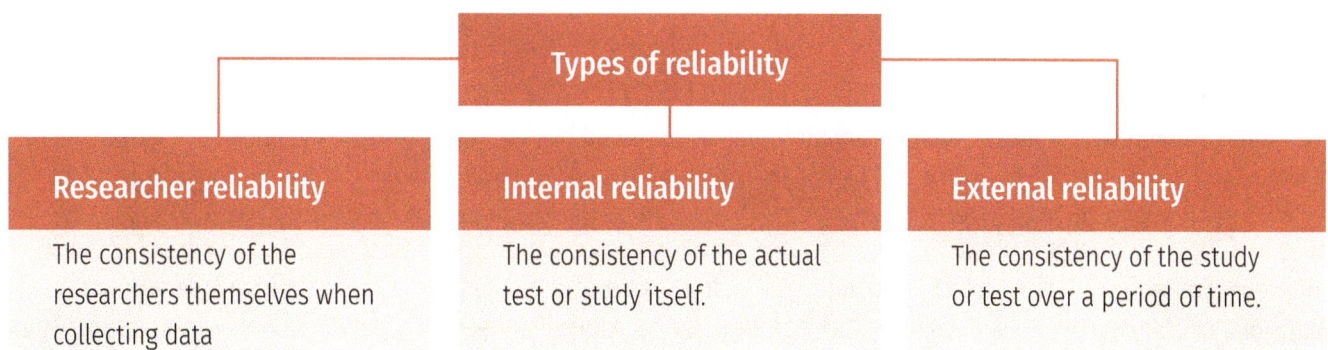

Types of reliability		
Researcher reliability	**Internal reliability**	**External reliability**
The consistency of the researchers themselves when collecting data	The consistency of the actual test or study itself.	The consistency of the study or test over a period of time.

Researcher reliability

Researcher reliability refers to the consistency of the researchers themselves when collecting data. In experiments, if the experimenter is consistent we say there is **experimenter reliability**. In non-experimental research such as interviews (e.g. structured clinical interview) and observations (using behavioural categories/coding system) where more than one researcher is involved in collecting data, if the results show a high level of consistency, we say the study has **inter-interviewer reliability** (for interviews) and **inter-observer reliability** (for observations). You can use the term *inter-rater reliability* when referring to interviews or observations.

Internal reliability

Internal reliability refers to how consistent *all the* questions or items in a test are in measuring the same behaviour or mental processes under investigation (e.g. personality types, IQ, depression). Are they all designed to measure the same thing? For a test to be reliable, the participants should always give a similar answer if it is repeated. For example, all the questions on a personality test should all be measuring the same thing (about personality). If it does, we say it has *internal reliability.*

External reliability

External reliability refers to whether the study or the instrument itself is consistent over different times. For example, if a person completes a personality test on a Friday and then repeats the same test two weeks later, and gets a similar score, we say it has *external reliability*.

Assessing and improving researcher reliability

Experiments

Assessing reliability. The reliability of an experiment researcher can be assessed by **replication** (repeating) of the experiment to see if the results are consistent; if so then there is researcher reliability.

Improving reliability. Careful planning, designing and conduct (e.g. procedures, material, and standardised instructions) will help to minimise experimenter bias and improve researcher reliability.

Self reports

Assessing reliability. The reliability of a single researcher conducting a questionnaire or interview can be assessed by the test-retest technique (see below). If the scores remain similar, then there is researcher reliability. Where there is more than one researcher, this can be assessed by comparing each other 's score to see if they are similar. If the results recorded show an agreed level of consistency (e.g. 80% or more) we say the results have *high inter-interviewer reliability*.

Improving reliability. Reliability can be improved through careful training of the researcher(s) on how to carry out the procedure (e.g. the use of standardised instructions) or how the study should be conducted. Running a pilot study to help identify and minimise investigator effect or error will help improve the reliability of the study.

Observations

Assessing reliability. The reliability of observations can be assessed by having two or more observers using the behavioural checklist/coding system. The scores are compared to see if they are similar. If the data from the different observers shows a high level of consistency (e.g. 0.8+), we say that the observers have *high inter-observer reliability*.

Improving reliability. If inter-observer reliability is low, this may be due to the operational definitions (behavioural categories/coding system) being unclear which can lead to confusion when recording the data, or the observers may not be using the behaviour checklist/coding system correctly. Inter-observer reliability can be improved through training the observers in the use of a behaviour checklist/coding system. Training will include discussing, clarifying and agreeing on the operational definitions of behaviours; observers must be clear exactly what they are looking for so it is recorded in the same way. Practice sessions where recorded behavioural sequences are watched, scored and then discussed until agreement is reached help improve reliability.

Assessing and improving internal and external reliability

Experimental research
Assessing internal and external reliability. An important way to assess the internal reliability of experimental research findings is through **replication**—repeating the study. Another researcher repeats the same laboratory conditions and procedures as the original study to see whether similar results occur. It is more difficult to assess or establish the reliability of findings from field and natural experiments because it is very hard to replicate the same conditions and procedures as in the original study, making it difficult to achieve the same result.

Improving internal and external reliability. If the results are conflicting, the design of the study will need to be carefully assessed, such as looking at the procedures and material to see whether confounding variables played a part (e.g. experimental bias, demand characteristics). The use of standardised instructions, experimental designs (e.g. use of random assignment and counter-balancing) or the use of a blind or double-blind procedure will minimise experimenter bias and demand characteristics, helping to improve the internal reliability of experiments.

Self-report techniques
Assessing internal reliability. To assess the internal reliability the **split-half technique** is used. This involves administering the questionnaire/test to a participant in two separate halves: for example, the odd-numbered questions then even-numbered questions. The scores for each half are compared. If the scores of both tests are similar (showing high positive correlation, 0.8+ (80%), the questionnaire/test is viewed as being reliable.

Assessing external reliability. To assess the external reliability of questionnaires or tests over time, the **test – retest technique** is used. The test is given to the participants at a certain time and repeated later with the same participants. If the scores obtained at both times are similar (strong positive correlation) the test is said to be reliable.

Improving internal and external reliability. If the questionnaire/test does not produce consistent results (i.e. test–retest shows a low correlation between the two sets of questions), the researcher will need to check the consistency on specific questions or items carefully and identify the parts that did not correlate well on the two occasions the test was given (which are weakening the reliability). This may require some questions or items to be modified or removed to improve the reliability. Once this is done, a retest is carried out to see if the reliability has improved. This process is repeated until a high level of test–retest reliability is shown by a strongly correlated first and second running of the questionnaire/test. The aim is to improve the internal reliability of a particular questionnaire or test so that the split-half correlation is at least 0.8+, showing a strong positive correlation, and thus good internal reliability is established.

Validity
As well as reliability, another important concept for all research methods is validity. Validity refers to how well a study or test measures what it claims to measure and the extent to which the findings can be generalised beyond the research setting. There are different types of validity by which a study can be assessed:

Internal validity
Internal validity refers to the extent the actual study or test correctly measures what it claims to measure. ("does what it says on the tin" so to speak). The internal validity can be applied to all research methods, although it is commonly applied to experimental design/procedures.

Experimental research

Assessing the internal validity of experiments. An experiment can have high or low internal validity. An experiment that is well designed, where unwanted variables or influences (extraneous variables) are controlled allowing us to be certain that the IV really caused the changes to the DV, we describe as having *high internal validity*. If a study leaves us with possible alternative interpretations (other variables) that caused the changes in the DV (i.e. the behaviour) then it is said to have *lower internal validity*. Poorly designed experiments (with a design flaw) can result in low internal validity. A small-scale pilot study will allow you to assess the design of your study. Feedback from the participants on the procedure or experimental task, including whether they guessed the hypothesis of the investigation, will help you improve and make adjustments to increase the internal validity of the experiment.

Improving internal validity of experiments. This involves the careful planning and design of the study; carrying out a pilot study will help minimise or control the influences of extraneous variables. This will ensure that the study is highly controlled and therefore results in fewer reasons to doubt that any effect observed is due to poor design and is not attributed to the change in the IV. The use of standardised instructions, experimental designs (e.g. use of random assignment and counter-balancing) or the use of a blind or double-blind procedure will minimise experimenter bias and demand characteristics. It will also offer greater control over unwanted variables and help improve the internal validity of the experiments.

Non-experimental research

Internal validity can also be applied to self-report techniques that measure certain psychological behaviour (e.g. questionnaires, tests, clinical structured interviews). Do these 'tools' measure what they are intended to measure? There are several types of validity that we can use to assess such techniques:

- **Face validity.** Assess the validity by looking at the questions/items to see if they look like what the test is supposed to measure. E.g., if a psychologist wants to examine the relationship between IQ and aggression, then all the questions in the test should relate directly to these two concepts – and nothing else. If the test appears to measure what it intended, then we say it has face validity.

- **Concurrent validity.** When a new test is under consideration, it is often assessed by comparison with a similar, established test that aims to measure the same thing. Both tests are given to the same participants and the two scores are correlated. The more positive the correlation, the stronger the similarity between the scores of the two tests and the greater the concurrent validity.

- **Predictive (criterion) validity.** This is used to assess the validity of a test in terms of how well it is able to predict the outcomes of people's behaviour. For example, a high score in a personality test may suggest that someone with a 'Type A' personality is more prone to heart disease. If at a later date that person does suffer a heart attack, then we can say that the test has predictive validity.

Assessing and improving the internal validity of self-reports. For self-report methods a pilot study could be used to evaluate the construction of the questions/test to see if it is appropriate. Based on the respondents' feedback, the necessary improvements can be made (such as avoiding difficult, confusing, leading questions) to ensure that the questions are understood in the same way by all the respondents. Any question that can lead to misunderstanding will affect the reliability and validity; as a result, some questions will be amended or omitted.

Assessing and improving the internal validity of observational research. In terms of observational research, the internal validity can be affected by **observer bias**. One way to assess this is to use more than one researcher to make the observations. They may use the same behavioural checklist to see how well their scores agree or disagree. The use of electronic devices, such as camcorders and audio recordings, is one way to increase the validity (and reliability) of observational research.

External validity

External validity is concerned with **generalisability**. External validity refers to the extent to which the tests can be generalised beyond the research setting, such as to other situations like the real world, other periods of time and other people. This can apply to both experimental and non-experimental research.

Experimental and non-experimental research

Assessing the external validity. We can assess the external validity of a study in various ways:

- **Population validity (sample).** Can the findings obtained from the research sample be generalised to the wider population or to a different culture? If, for example, a study used a sample of 15 male university students, can we go beyond the findings extracted from these students and apply them to other groups in society or populations – such as elderly men or women of any age? A limited sample may not be representative of the general wider population, and therefore may have low population validity.

- **Ecological validity (settings).** This refers to whether the findings of a study can be generalised to human behaviour in the real world. Studies that examine behaviour in a natural setting (e.g. naturalistic observation) are said to have high ecological validity – the findings have relevance to real life. But those that take place under controlled (artificial) conditions, such as laboratory experiments are said to be low in ecological validity.

- **Temporal validity (times).** Refers to the ability to generalise the findings of the study to other time periods (and not just when the study was conducted). For example, are the findings of past studies that were conducted in the 1960s, such as Milgram's obedience study, valid in today's society? Equally, for a present study can we apply the findings to the past? If so, we say it has temporal validity.

Improving external validity. In terms of experiments, one way to improve the external (ecological) validity is to try to carry out the experiment (if possible) in a more naturalistic setting, such as a field experiment. If this is not possible, the ecological validity can be improved by making the situation or task more realistic, called **mundane realism** in the experiment. This is when the research setting reflects a real-life setting.

With all types of research methods, temporal and population validity can be improved by taking a larger sample or a more varied sample, such as including a wider or different age group, or carrying out the study in a different culture or geographical region, for example.

The relationship between validity and reliability

The findings of research can be *reliable* – but not *valid*. A study that consistently produces the same results when it is repeated does not necessarily mean it reflects an accurate picture of what it *set out* to investigate. For example, a group of students used a questionnaire to investigate the drinking behaviour of their teachers on weekdays. The results showed that one out of 50 teachers said that they drank during the week. Is this likely to be a true reflection of their drinking behaviour? It is possible that the teachers lied on the questionnaire because they were afraid that the students would disapprove of their drinking habits. The students might administer the questionnaire on other occasions and the teachers may continue to lie, thus producing the same false results consistently. Such findings are *reliable*, but they lack validity because the study failed to find out about the teachers' real drinking habits.

1. A psychology teacher wondered whether there was a relationship between internet use and sociability. The teacher decided to investigate this by asking volunteers from the sixth forms of several local schools to keep a diary. Each volunteer recorded in a diary the number of hours spent using the internet over a four-week period. At the end of four weeks, all the participants were given a test to measure their sociability. A high score on this test indicates that someone is very sociable.

   a) Describe how the teacher could have assessed the reliability of this study. . . . . **(3 marks)**

   b) What is meant by internal validity? . . . . **(1 marks)**

   c) Describe how the teacher could have assessed the internal validity of the sociability test. . . . **(3 marks)**

2. A pilot study has indicated that boys and girls play differently. Boys have been shown to engage more in rough and tumble play (e.g. pushing, hitting) and girls have been shown to engage in more co-operative play (e.g. clapping games, skipping games). A psychologist wished to study the differences between boys' and girls' play in primary schools. She asked the head teachers of several schools for permission to observe children playing. She observed the children from a window and recorded the ways in which boys and girls were playing.

   a) Explain what is meant by the term 'reliability' in the context of this study. . . . . **(2 marks)**

   b) Explain two ways in which the reliability of the observations of boys and girls playing could have been improved. . . . . **(2 marks)**

   c) Explain how two factors might have affected the validity of this study. . . . . **(2 marks + 2 marks)**

The AQA specification: A-LEVEL ONLY

- Features of science: objectivity and the empirical method; replicability and falsifiability; theory construction and hypothesis testing; paradigms and paradigm shifts

The exam requires that you are able to:

▶ Describe the key features of science (replicability, objectivity, theory construction, hypothesis testing).

Key terms

- **Science:** a procedure used (i.e. the scientific method) to seek and obtain valid and reliable knowledge about the world we live in with the aim of being able to understand, explain, predict and control the world around us.

- **Scientific method:** the research process that scientists follow to gather valid and reliable knowledge; by observing a phenomenon; formulating a testable hypothesis, collecting data using empirical research and drawing a conclusion from the data.

  As a note, 'scientific method' is not to be confused with 'scientific methods' (plural), which refers to the different 'tool' used (e.g. experiments, observation, questionnaires, correlational analysis) to collect data.

- **Objectivity:** a view that scientific research and evidence must be free of (not influenced by) the researcher's own private values, opinions, expectations and bias.

- **Empiricism:** the view that information collected (e.g. data) to develop or support a theory can only be obtained from what is directly observable through our senses.

- **Empirical methods:** (or empirical research) refers to the types of research methods that enable the researcher to collect information or data that derives directly from our senses, such as using experiment, observation, questionnaires, interviews, psychological tests and case studies.

- **Replicability:** (replication) being able to repeat a study in exactly the same manner as the original study to see if similar results are found.

- **Falsification principle:** any hypothesis/theory that is tested must have the ability to be proven wrong using empirical methods.

- **Hypothesis testing:** as the name suggests, this means testing the hypothesis by designing an empirical research study to examine whether it is right or wrong (falsifiable) as indicated by the data collected.

- **Theory construction:** refers to how theories are developed and tested through the scientific method (inductive and deductive approach) in order to explain an observed phenomenon.

Definition and goals of science

- **Science** refers to a type of method of research used to acquire valid and reliable information about the natural and social world. Science also has a set of goals which aim to be able to describe, explain, predict and control the world around us – in other words, how the world works. Physics, chemistry and biology are referred to as the 'natural sciences' whereas psychology, sociology and economics are called the 'social sciences'. What they have in common is that both groups use the scientific method of investigation when constructing theories (explanations). Psychology is generally viewed as a science as it attempts to study behaviour (actions and responses) and mental processes (thoughts and feelings) using the scientific method. Many of the topics that you have studied at AS and A2 level have been investigated using the scientific method (memory, stress, relationships etc.).

Below are the four goals that the psychologist as a scientist (and all scientists) aims to achieve when studying behaviour and the mind:

- **Description** – the first goal of science is to *describe* the phenomenon observed by giving an account of it by naming, classifying, identifying or detailing what is being observed. In terms of psychology, the researcher may attempt to describe the behaviour and mental processes they are interested in. For example, they may have noticed some infants display clingy behaviour towards their mothers while others do not.

- **Explain** – the next goal of science is to be able to *explain* the phenomena (the 'why' question). In terms of psychology, the researcher attempts to explain the causes of behaviours and mental processes – why this is happening. For example, Mary Ainsworth (1978) suggests infants who display clingy behaviour towards their mothers have an insecure attachment (i.e. emotional insecurity) because the mother has provided inconsistent or neglectful care towards the infant (known as the *maternal sensitivity explanation*).

- **Prediction** – once explanations are given, scientists can then go on and attempt to *predict* (hypothesise) when this phenomenon is likely to occur—under what conditions/context. For example, psychologists can predict when an insecure child-mother attachment is likely to occur (e.g. infant or mother is hospitalised, the death of the mother, institutional care, day-care and so on). They can also predict that insecure attachment may cause emotional problems later on in life (e.g. poor relationships in adulthood) as predicted by Bowlby.

- **Control** – finally, if the scientist can predict an event, they can then move onto the next stage: the ability to *control* that phenomenon—what causes something to occur. In the context of psychology, 'control' means manipulating/altering certain factors or conditions that affect the behaviour in order to bring about a desired outcome. The aim is to bring an improvement in the quality of life in humans. For example, we can 'intervene' in the quality of parenting by offering parenting intervention programmes aimed at improving the infant-mother attachment relationship.

The major features of science

For a discipline such as biology, physics or psychology to be classified as a 'science' the **scientific method** of research must be applied when gathering knowledge. Below are the main features of the scientific method:

Objectivity

- Scientists are required to be *objective* when carrying out research. This means that the researcher's own private values, opinions, emotions, expectations, political bias and religious views should not influence or contaminate the research at any stage (from beginning to end). The researcher remains 'unbiased' and 'neutral' in the research process. This means that any theory or explanation that has been carried in an objective manner will be trusted more than research that is subjective, or biased.

Example of objectivity

Psychologists can attempt to be objective when conducting research. For example, they can use strategies such as the double-blind procedure in experiments, when the researcher and the participants are both kept in the dark about the true aim of the experiment in order to eliminate any possible bias and expectations (whether 'intentional' or 'unintentional') the researcher may have. The use of standardisation instructions and procedure in the study means all the participants are instructed in the same way and tested under the same conditions; again the psychologist is striving for objectivity. In the process of sampling, the psychologists can select research participants using a computer program to generate a random sample, to avoid biasing factors (age, gender, beauty, friends, etc.). Researchers usually make their measurements with instruments (e.g. psychological tests, questionnaires, content analysis and observational techniques - behavioural categories) in order to maintain objectivity.

Empiricism

- *Empiricism* is the essential element of the scientific method. Empiricism basically means that the information collected (e.g. data) to develop/support a theory can only be obtained directly from our senses. The term **empirical evidence** (*or empirical data*) means information that is collected using the empirical methods of investigation. **Empirical method** refers to the type of methods used to collected empirical evidence such as experiments (lab, field, natural), observational techniques (naturalistic, controlled),questionnaires, interviews, psychological tests and case studies. The use of empirical methods is important in the scientific research process because other researchers can repeat the study to check the reliability or validity of the findings. This means all other information that is based on speculation, intuition, reasoning, common sense, belief, faith or old wives, tales is excluded as unscientific!

Example of empiricism

Most of the studies you have learnt in AS Psychology are based on collecting empirical evidence. For example in the topic on Memory, the Peterson and Peterson experiment on duration (how long information remains in STM without verbal rehearsal) collected data from the participants' test, which helped them draw conclusions about the duration in STM. Another example is Ainsworth's strange situation study where she collected data based on observations to test and classify the different types of attachment that exist between a mother and infant. However, not all psychology theory is based on empiricism. If you recall, the psychodynamic explanation (Freud's theory) for psychopathology is based on concepts such as the 'unconscious', 'ego', 'superego' and 'oral stage' which cannot be tested either by observation or experimentation. This makes his theory unscientific because it is not supported by empirical evidence.

How do psychologists collect empirical evidence?

Psychologists can investigate human behaviour empirically through collecting data on people they are researching. The data gathered is classified as empirical evidence. Data is collected via the different research methods and techniques such as observational techniques, experimentations, interviews, questionnaires and psychological tests. Some empirical evidence may be directly observable to the researcher such as when carrying out observational studies or experimentation (and quantitative data is collected, e.g. scores). At other times, human behaviour may be 'invisible' to the researcher — not directly observable to our senses. So the researcher may use a questionnaire to collect data on a person's preferences, attitudes and beliefs that would otherwise be indirectly observable to the psychologists.

Replicability

- Another key feature of the scientific research method is *replication*. That is, the ability for another researcher to **repeat** a study in exactly the same manner as the original study to see if similar results are found. This means all the details of the original study need to be clearly reported (e.g. procedures and results). Replication allows us to see if the original findings were deliberately manipulated by the researcher (fraud) or the results were a one-off. More importantly replication allows us to see if the results are consistent (i.e.**reliable**). If the repeated findings are reliable this would give validity to the theory they support. If a study cannot reproduce the same result then the theory may have little value. Therefore research findings must be replicated before they are incorporated into the body of scientific knowledge.

- Some research methods, such as controlled laboratory experiments, are easier to replicate than others. That is why the findings from laboratory experiments tend to be more reliable. It is more difficult to replicate a study that is carried out in natural settings, such as in fields, or through natural experiments and naturalistic observations because it is difficult to achieve the same conditions as in the original study. The results can therefore be unreliable in these types of research methods.

Example of replication

The research findings into the capacity of short-term memory (STM) suggest that we can hold between five and nine items. This is because the studies were based on laboratory experiments, which has meant the original study can be replicated by other researchers, using the same experimental conditions and procedures, to see if they get similar results. Their results were indeed similar, proving that our explanation of the capacity of short-term memory is valid.

Falsification principle

- Another main feature of science is the *falsification principle*. Karl Popper (1902-1994) argued that for a theory to be classified as 'scientific' it must meet the criteria of falsification. This means the theory must be capable of being proved wrong (falsified). Scientific research requires that any theory/hypothesis that is tested must always have the 'ability' to be incorrect empirically (through observation or experimentation). Any theory that cannot be proven wrong empirically does not meet the criteria of science and therefore is not classified as scientific knowledge. Falsification is important as it allows the ability for the theory to be modified, revised and improved upon, which is a hallmark of a good scientific practice.

Example of falsification

For example, we can test the hypothesis, 'all ravens are black' empirically. If, however, we find a 'white raven' we can challenge this statement and say it is not a scientific truth—the hypothesis has been falsified. The point is not whether all ravens are black or not, but the fact that the hypothesis met the criteria of the falsification principle through empirical observation. Some critics argue that the study of parapsychology is a pseudoscience (not a real science) because many of the explanations and research evidence are beyond being falsified. For example, a psychic who is asked to demonstrate his powers in a controlled laboratory setting and subsequently cannot do so may offer numerous explanations, such as the scepticism of the researchers interferes with the 'psychic forces';or the time of the day is wrong or the subject was just having a bad day, etc. The psychic wins either way. His powers are proven when he demonstrates evidence of psychic ability, but his powers are not disproved when he does not. This inability of some psychical research to be proven wrong, under Popper's definition, would be deemed unscientific knowledge.

Consider Freud's theory about repression. The assumption is that psychological problems (e.g. depression, neurosis) of adults are rooted in childhood trauma. If the adult can recall and describe the childhood trauma, then Freud's theory will conclude that his or her current problems developed because of that early trauma. If the adult cannot recall any trauma, then the theory concludes that he or she has repressed the events into his or her unconscious mind. This hypothesis cannot be proven wrong.

Theory construction

The main purpose of scientific research is to collect data to *construct* (develop) theories, as well as to continue to test existing theories in order to strengthen, modify or reject them. A theory is a set of inter-related (connected) explanations of a phenomenon that has been observed. Theories can be constructed in two ways: through the processes of *inductive* research, and by *deductive research*. In reality both approaches work together in a complementary manner of theory construction and testing. With inductive research, initial observations are made and a theory is developed from them, whereas a deductive process generates a hypothesis/theory which is then tested by experiments and observations.

Inductive research

The inductive approach puts theory construction at the end of the research process:

Step 1:   **Observation** – initially an observation is made of a specific phenomenon where a pattern or trend has been identified.

E.g. A scientist finds that if a particular part of the brain is stimulated with electrodes the person often experiences an 'out-of-body sensation', i.e. seeing themselves while floating above the ground.

Step 2:   **Carry out study** – the next stage is for the scientist to carry out a study to collect data on the observed phenomenon using empirical methods. The scientist will analyse the results to see if they can find a pattern or trend in the data.

E.g. Data is collected from case studies, questionnaires and interviews with patients who have an outer-body experience when a specific part of the brain is stimulated.

Step 3:   **Develop theory** – if enough information/data is accumulated to demonstrate a pattern or trend then a theory will be constructed to provide an explanation for the observed phenomenon. If the data does not support the theory, the theory is rejected or modified.

E.g. Outer-body experiences are not real and can be explained by the malfunctioning of electrical activity or malfunctioning of the temporal-parietal junction(TPJ) in the brain.

Inductive research is particularly useful when psychologists are beginning to investigate a new area where no existing theory has been developed. The inductive process provides a theoretical framework which can, if it seems appropriate, be investigated further using the deductive approach (see below), which is more akin to theory testing than theory construction.

The inductive approach to theory construction

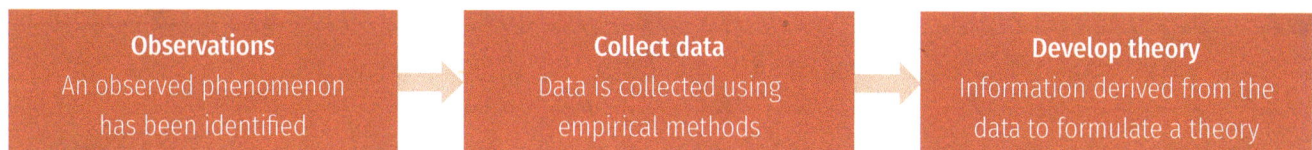

Observations	**Collect data**	**Develop theory**
An observed phenomenon has been identified	Data is collected using empirical methods	Information derived from the data to formulate a theory

Deductive research

Deductive research (known as the *hypothetico-deductive approach*) is recognised as the 'scientific method' of research investigation. The deductive approach puts theory construction at the beginning of the research study. The researcher then investigates this by formulating a *hypothesis* derived from theory that they can test. Initially, the theory may be an existing theory that is based on research carried out by others or it may have developed through the inductive process — by observation. Either way, hypothesis testing allows the validity of the theory to be strengthened or the theory to be rejected. It also allows the theory to be tested further, under different conditions, enabling us to refine and revise the theory, and thus expanding our scientific knowledge.

Step 1:   **Theory development** – a theory may be formulated based on observations of a particular phenomenon—a pattern or trend has been identified, or an aspect of an existing theory is being tested based on previous research studies.

Step 2:   **Hypothesis testing** – the scientist then formulates a hypothesis to test that it is derived from the theory. The hypothesis makes a prediction to see what will happen in a particular situation.

Step 3:   **Carry out study** – the scientists then carry out a study (using empirical methods) in which the hypothesis is testable and falsifiable.

Step 4:   **Draw conclusion** – if the results support the hypothesis (assuming replication has been achieved and the study was designed well), a new theory is developed, or an existing theory is strengthened or modified to accommodate the new findings. If the results do not support the hypothesis, this can lead to the theory being challenged (rejected) and an alternative theory being provided.

The research process does not have an end. When the results support the hypothesis, additional hypotheses are developed to test the theory further under different conditions. If new supporting evidence is found the theory is modified and further hypothesis testing is carried out, and so the whole process is repeated again and again—in a cycle.

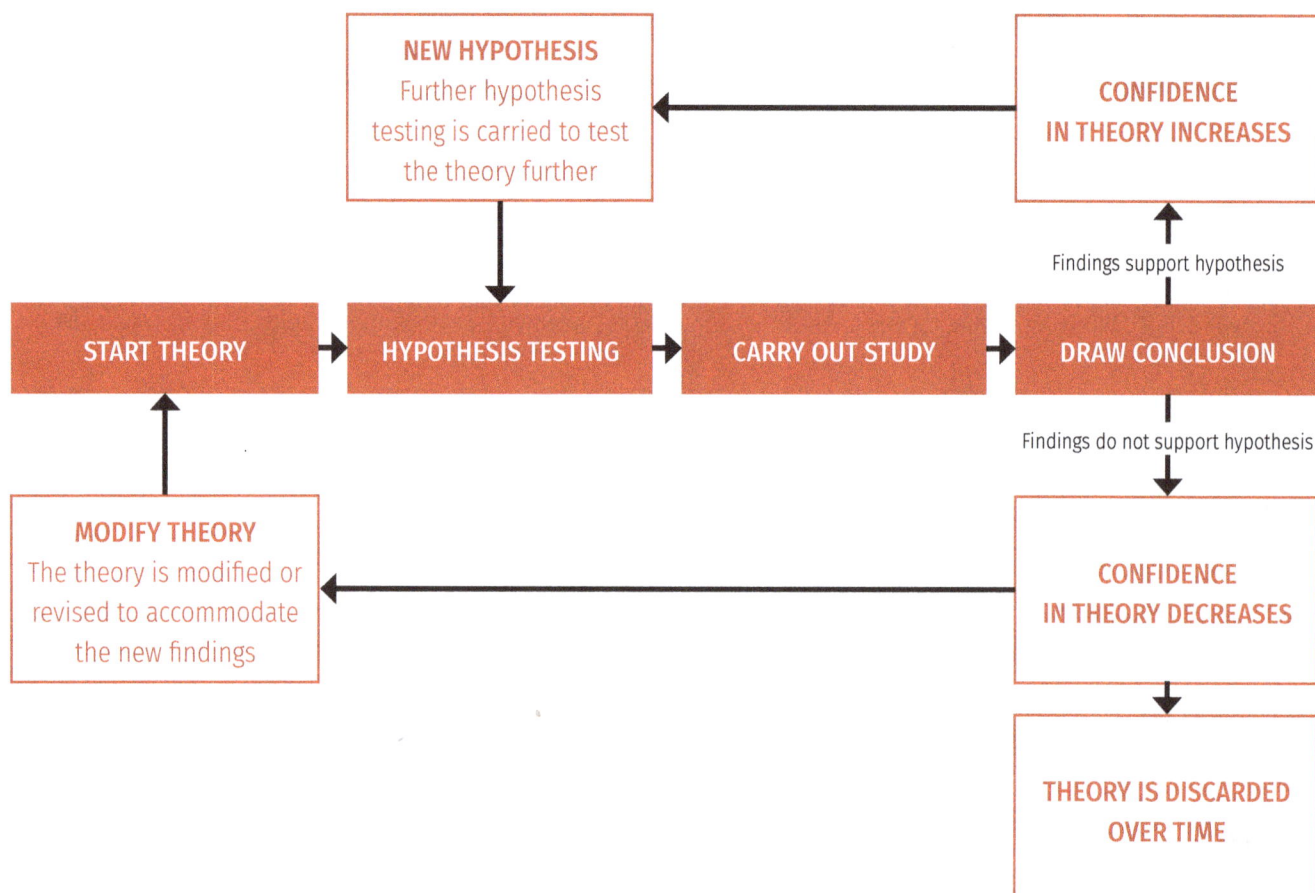

Theory construction.

A good theory will generate a number of testable hypotheses. In a typical study only one or a few of these hypotheses can be evaluated. If the evidence supports the hypotheses, confidence in the theory they were derived from generally grows. If the hypotheses are not supported, confidence in the theory decreases, and revision to the theory may be made to accommodate new findings. If the hypotheses generated by a theory consistently fail to provide support for the theory, the theory may be discarded. Thus theory construction and testing is a gradual process.

Hypothesis testing

- Scientific research often starts off by identifying a topic of interest to be tested, which may be based on observation or to test an existing theory. A hypothesis is developed to test the observed phenomenon/theory. A hypothesis is a precise, testable statement that involves making a prediction about the expected outcome of the study. *Hypothesis testing,* as the name suggests, aims to test the hypothesis by designing a research study by which the hypothesis can be proven right or wrong (falsified) empirically.

Hypothesis testing is an important element in research as it helps us to develop a theory or strengthen, revise or reject existing theories. We need to ensure that the variables are clearly **operational** in measurable terms when we test a hypothesis. In hypothesis testing there are two opposing hypotheses that are being tested: the *alternative hypothesis* (Ha) and the *null hypothesis* (Ho). For example, take the study below about whether sugary drinks have an effect on a memory recall test:

- **Null hypothesis** – The null hypothesis is a statement of prediction that the results will *show no relationship* or *no difference* between the variables. For example:
  There will be no difference in a recall word test between participants who drink sugary drinks from those who do not consume a sugary drink.

- **Alternative hypothesis** – The alternative hypothesis is one in which there is a difference (or an effect) between two or more variables as predicted by the researchers. For example:
  Participants who drink sugary drinks will do better in a recall word test and those who do not drink sugary drinks.

In hypothesis testing you will test to see which of the hypotheses will be accepted and which will be rejected. If the *alternative hypothesis* is correct (the findings support your prediction) then you would reject the null hypothesis. However, if the alternative hypothesis was not supported in the findings, then you would accept the null hypothesis and reject the alternative hypothesis. Deciding which hypothesis to accept requires a statistical test to analyse the data. If the results support the hypothesis, the theory gains credibility. If the results do not support the hypothesis, this suggests the theory is incorrect or needs modification/revising.

A little bit more information on the 'null hypothesis'

Psychologists must initially assume when carrying out an investigation that there is no relationship between the variables (e.g. sugary drinks and memory recall). It is the job of the alternative hypothesis to prove that there is a relationship and thus prove that the null hypothesis is wrong. Therefore in a research study there are really two hypotheses that are being tested: the null hypothesis and the alternative hypothesis (so-called because it is an alternative to the null hypothesis).

Exam Questions

1. Explain what is meant by the term 'replication' in research investigation and why replication is an important feature of scientific research. . . . . **(2 marks + 3 marks)**

2. Explain what is meant by the term 'objectivity' in research investigation. . . . . **(2 marks)**

3. Explain what is meant by the term 'hypothesis testing' in research investigation. . . . . **(2 marks)**

4. Explain what is meant by the term 'theory construction' in research investigation. . . . . **(2 marks)**

Some people believe they have 'psychic' abilities, such as telepathy. We can define telepathy as the ability to acquire the thoughts of another person (i.e. what they are thinking about) without having any physical or verbal contact with them. Many studies into telepathy are now held in tightly controlled conditions that can be easily repeated by other psychologists. For example, to test the existence of telepathy a participant looks at an image that has been randomly selected by a computer, while the person who claims to have psychic abilities attempts to pick the same image in another room. Some sceptics argue telepathy does not exist because it does not really meet the criteria of scientific investigation and therefore falls under the term pseudoscience (false science).

5. Explain why the above study of telepathy does meets the criteria of scientific investigation. Refer to some of the major features of science in your answer. . . . . **(6 marks)**

The AQA specification: A-LEVEL ONLY

- Reporting psychological investigations. Sections of a scientific report: abstract, introduction, method, results, discussion and referencing.

The exam requires that you are able to:

▶ Describe the conventions for reporting psychological investigations, including how the report is structured (format).

Introduction

Once a research study has been completed, the next stage for the researcher is to share his/her findings with other psychologists. This will require the researcher to write up the study before sending it for peer review and possibly for publication in a scientific journal. There are certain conventions (guidelines) that should be followed when writing a psychological research (otherwise known as a 'Research Report'). The purpose of following this format is so the researcher can be conveyed in a clear and precise manner, so it is easier to understand. Below provides outline of the format on how the psychological report should be presented.

The layout of a psychological research report

The standard format of a research paper in a journal consists of the following elements:

Title:	tells the reader what the research is investigating
Abstract:	provides the reader with a short summary of the study
Introduction:	provides the reader the background literature and rationale of the study
Method:	describe how the study was carried out
Results:	to summarise the findings
Discussion:	to discuss the findings and their implications
References:	to inform the readers about allthe sources of information the researcher used
Appendices:	additional material that would interrupt the flow of the research report

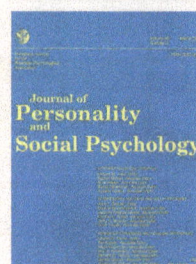

Conventions for reporting psychological investigations

Title

A research report begins with a title page. This needs to be clear and precise (usually 12-15 words) as to what the research is investigating. This is important because anyone who reads it will know exactly what the report is about before they decide to read further.

Abstract

This is a short summary of the whole study (about 150 to 200 words). The report covers the aims/hypothesis, introduction, method/procedures, results and the conclusion. Although the abstract appears first it is usually written after all the other sections have been written—last.

Introduction

The introduction really includes three sections, although these are not identified by separate headings. The opening explains why it is interesting and/or important and the reason for carrying out this study. Next is the literature review; this gives the reader background information on previous studies and theories relevant to the research study. However, the literature review is not simply a list of past studies. Instead, provides an argument/reason for why the research question is worth addressing (it may have methodological problems, or perhaps scope for extending it or it may simply replicating the study). The final paragraph, the researcher need to state the hypothesis—what you intended the outcome of your study will be (e.g. participants who studied in the presence of music will recall significantly more words than participants who studied in silence).

Methods

The method section is where the researcher describes how they conducted your study. It should be clear and detailed enough that other researchers could replicate the study by following your 'recipe'. One way to improve the clarity is to split the method section in 3 or 4 subdivisions: Design, Participants, Materials/Stimuli and Procedure. A method might include a number of sections. Below is what a 'typical' method section might include:

Design —This states the chosen research method used: experimental or non-experimental (survey, observation, content analysis, or correlational analysis). If an experiment was car ried out; it will need to state the conditions (e.g. experimental and control group) and how the participants were assigned to the different groups — the experimental design used (i.e. repeated measures, independent group design or matched pairs). Need to state clearly how the variables were manipulated and measured and what controls were in place (e.g. standard instructions; random assignment; counter-balancing; double-blind technique; environment; time of day).

Participants —In this section, information about the participants are described such as the sampling technique and recruitment used (e.g. advertisement for a volunteer sample), the number, age and breakdown of gender should also be stated, and it may also be appropriate where the research was conducted and from what country the participants came.

Apparatus/materials —In this section, the researcher include the materials they needed in order to carry out their research. E.g.: computers, video/audio stimuli, consent forms, standardised instructions; tasks; response sheets; questionnaires, interview schedules; or observation schedule.

Procedure —This section of the report describes a step-by-step how the investigation was carried out—what the participants did and in the order it happened. Sufficient details needs to be provided so others researchers can replicate the study. You will need to include where it took place and instructions given to the participants before (e.g. consents form), during (standardised instructions) and after (debriefing) the study.

Results

This section is where the results are presented—what the researchers found; it should be a summary of data. They typically include *descriptive statistics*; this is when the data is summarised by using the appropriate tables, averages and graphs. Then there is the *inferential statistics*; a statistical test to determine how significant the results are—whether they hypothesis has been accepted or rejected.

Discussion

The discussion mainly explains what the results show. This covers a number of elements (although they are not broken into subheading such as below)

(a)   *Summary of research—* Firstly, it begins with a summary of the study and provides a clear answer to the research question; whether the hypothesis is supported or rejected. The researcher then considers the relevance of the findings to existing theories and research evidence that they wrote in the introduction of their report (e.g. Do the results provide support for any existing theories/studies? If not, how can this be explained?).

(b)   *Theoretical implications*—Next, there is some discussion of the practical implications of the research. How can the results be used, and by whom, to accomplish some real-world application?

(c)   *Limitations*—This is followed by a discussion of the study's limitations by looking at the methodology and design which may have affected the validity of the study (e.g. Perhaps there is some evidence that participants did not fully understand their task) and how this could have been corrected.

(d)   *Suggestions for future research*—Most discussions end with some suggestions for future research. What *new* research questions has the study raised that could be investigated?

References

The final section is a reference list. The full details of any journal articles, books and websites that are mentioned in their report. This is very useful for those reading the report, as they may be interested to extend their reading to the articles and books indicated by the researchers who wrote the paper.

Appendices

An appendix is for additional material that would interrupt the flow of the research report if it were presented within any of the major sections. For example, in the appendices the researcher would place things like raw data, calculations, standard instructions, present lists of stimulus words, questionnaires, observation schedules and so on.

1. A psychologist was interested in testing a new treatment for people with eating disorders. She put up adverts in several London clinics to recruit participants. Thirty people came forward and they were all given a structured interview by a trained therapist. The therapist then calculated a numerical score for each participant as a measure of their current functioning, where 50 indicates excellent, healthy functioning and zero indicates failure to function adequately. The psychologist then randomly allocated half the participants to a treatment group and half to a no-treatment group. After eight weeks, each participant was re-assessed using a structured interview conducted by the same trained therapist, and given a new numerical score. The trained therapist did not know which participants had been in either group. For each participant, the psychologist calculated an improvement score by subtracting the score at the start of the study from the score after eight weeks. The greater the number, the better the improvement.

Table 1: **Median and range of improvement scores for the treatment group and for the non-treatment group**

	Treatment group	Non-treatment group
Median	10.9	2.7
Range	2.1	0.8

The psychologist noticed that female and male participants seemed to have responded rather differently to the treatment. She decided to test the following hypothesis:

Female patients with an eating disorder will show greater improvement in their symptoms after treatment with the new therapy than male patients.

She used a new set of participants and, this time, used self-report questionnaires instead of interviews with a therapist.

a) Imagine that you are writing up the report for this study.
What is the purpose of the introduction section of a report? . . . . **(2 marks)**

b) Imagine that you are the psychologist and are writing up the report of the study.
Write an appropriate methods section which includes reasonable detail of design, participants, materials and procedure. Make sure that there is enough detail to allow another researcher to carry out this study in the future. . . . . **(10 marks)**

· design

· participants

· materials

· procedures

The AQA specification:

- Quantitative and qualitative data; the distinction between qualitative and quantitative data collection techniques.
- Primary and secondary data

The exam requires that you are able to:

▶ Understand what is meant by primary and secondary data, and quantitative and qualitative data.
▶ Understand the different ways of evaluating research methods..

Research methods

What is the point of doing psychological research?

The purpose of any psychological research study is to collect information (often referred to as 'data') in order get a better understanding of people's behaviour. Psychologists do this by carrying out investigations called 'research studies' to collect evidence. Collecting information helps us to build up or challenge existing psychological knowledge (eg, theories and explanations) about our social behaviour/world. This can help make the world we live in a better place.

The different research methods psychologists use

Below are the different research methods that sociologists can use when carrying out an investigation:

- Experiments (field and laboratory experiments).
- Questionnaires (open-ended or close-ended).
- Interviews (structured or unstructured).
- Observations (structured or unstructured).
- Meta-analysis (data from a large number of studies).
- Documents (eg, diaries, letters, magazines, photographs, newspapers and television programmes).

Primary and secondary sources of data

When deciding on their research method (as listed above), sociologists have a choice of using either **primary** or **secondary** sources of data. *Primary data* is information that has been collected by the sociologists themselves for their own purpose. *Secondary data* is information that already exists and has been collected, usually by non-sociologists, with quite different purposes in mind to those of psychological researchers. This type of data may then be re-interpreted and re-analysed by psychologists for their own objectives. The table below shows which research methods use primary and secondary sources of data:

Primary sources of data
- Experiments
- Interviews
- Questionnaires
- Observations

Secondary sources of data
- Meta-analysis
- Documents

✓✗ Evaluation

Advantages and disadvantages of using primary data

✓ **Control over the research.**
The psychologists has complete control of their investigation, which means they can collect the information they want rather than using existing information that may not be completely relevant.

✓ **Original data.**
Often no secondary data exist on a particular issue, which means that the psychologists has no choice but to undertake their own research study.

✗ **Cost and time.**
Psychologists may not be able to carry out their own research investigation because doing so can be time-consuming and costly.

Advantages and disadvantages of using secondary data

✓ **Quick and cheap.**
Using secondary data is much cheaper and less time-consuming then carrying out your own research: the researcher does not have to spend money or time collecting their own information as it already exists.

✓ **Only source available.**
Existing secondary sources may be the only option available for psychologists. This is specially true if they are investigating something that has happened in the past.

✗ **Different purposes.**
Secondary information is collected by non-sociologists for very different purposes than those which psychologists have in mind. This means that a psychologists may find some of the information unsuitable for what they are trying to find out.

Qualitative and quantitative data

Psychologists may collect or use two types of data while carrying out a research study. We call these quantitative and qualitative data.

- **Quantitative data.** This refers to information collected in numerical form, that is, in numbers, often in statistics (eg, percentages, averages, tally scores, etc). Some research methods allow the findings gathered by the study to be easily quantified and expressed numerically. Research methods that collect quantitative data are referred to as **quantitative research methods.**

- **Qualitative data.** This refers to information that is collected in written words (and/or audio and video) rather than numerically. The purpose of gathering qualitative data is to provide a rich and detailed account of the participants' meanings, thoughts and experiences, allowing a deeper understanding of what they mean. Research methods that collect quantitative data are referred to as **qualitative research methods.**

Research methods that collect quantitative data

Primary sources
- Experiments
- Structured interviews
- Closed questionnaires
- Controlled observations

Secondary sources
- Official statistics

Research methods that collect qualitative data

Primary sources
- Unstructured interviews
- Open questionnaires
- Unstructured observations

Secondary sources
- Diaries, letters, newspapers, magazines

✓✗ Evaluation

Advantages and disadvantages of using quantitative data

✓ **Easy to analyse and interpret.**
An advantage of research methods that collect the information as quantitative data is that they allow the numbers to be quantified and summarised, which makes it easy to analyse and interpret the data to see if they identify patterns or causal links. This allows us to make generalisations about cause and effect in human behaviour, for example, that the amount of time young children spend playing violent video games leads to an increase in aggressive physical behaviour at school.

✗ **Time-consuming.**
A disadvantage of quantitative data is that it reduces thoughts and feelings to numbers, which limits a deeper understanding of human behaviour and experiences. Quantitative data cannot explain why people do things, just identify trends or relationships. For example, psychologists may find a relationship between middle-age men and high levels of suicide but fails to explain why middle-age men are more likely to commit suicide than other age groups.

Advantages and disadvantages of qualitative data

✓ **Deeper understanding.**
One advantage of research methods that collect qualitative data is that they provide a deeper understanding of human behaviour, such as experiences, values, attitudes and beliefs, that cannot be achieved by quantitative methods.

✗ **Time-consuming.**
One disadvantage of research methods that collect qualitative data is that information gathered is most often in written form, which is difficult to code, analyse and interpret. Therefore, it is less easy to form conclusions than when using quantitative data.

Meta-analysis

A research method that uses secondary data is known as meta-analysis. This method allows researchers to combine the findings of different studies (with the same research hypothesis and research method) and treat them as though they were one large study which gives us one overall results. By pooling data from multiple studies, this allows the researcher to arrive at an overall conclusion about the topic or issue studied.

Strength

Using meta-analysis is cheaper way to conduct your research as you do not have to pay expenses for carrying out an experiment. The results can provide strong evidence for the hypothesis which means they become more generalisable.

Weakness

Meta-analysis has a high chance of being prone to publication bias, this is where the researcher collecting the data will pick specific studies that only provide the outcome that the researcher is looking for. Therefore, the data will be bias becomes it only reflect some of the data and therefore the conclusion drawn may not be valid.

Reliability

- **Replication of method.** Reliability refers to the replicability of a research method to check if the findings are consistent. If the method used in a study can be easily repeated to check the results, we say it is a reliable method. Methods viewed as being easily replicable are:
  - close-ended questionnaires
  - structured interviews
  - controlled observations
  - experiments

The above methods are viewed as reliable because they are conducted and collect data in a structured way, that is, instructions, procedures, questions are all carried out in standardised and/or controlled conditions with little interpretation or involvement on the part of the researcher. This means another researcher can repeat the same standardised format as the original study to see whether similar results are found. The 'unstructured' methods such as open-ended questionnaires, unstructured interviews and participant observations are less reliable research methods. It is very hard to replicate studies using these techniques with the same questions, procedures and conditions as in the original study, given that these conditions are often unique, and therefore difficult to see whether they yield similar results.

- **Reliability of data.** Reliability also refers to how **consistent the findings (data)** are in the study. If the chosen method is easily replicable, we can also check the reliability of the findings. That is, if the study were to be carried out again by other sociologists on a similar or identical group of people and similar results were found, the findings would be said to be reliable. As noted, the 'structured' methods are easier to replicate, to see if the findings are reliable, than 'unstructured' methods.

It is important that the findings are reliable in order for the study to be trusted, so sociologists can make generalisations from them.

Exam advice

Please note: in exams, do not make absolute statements, for example, 'questionnaires are reliable' or 'observations are unreliable', as no research is 100% reliable or unreliable. Instead, write 'high' or 'low'. So, for example, you should say, 'It has been argued that questionnaires are high in reliability'. This is more of an evaluative comment.

Validity

- Another important aspect of evaluating any sociological research is validity. **Validity** refers to how accurate and true the findings of the study are. A study that is valid is one that produces a true picture of what it is aiming to investigate. If the research lacks validity, the researcher cannot ensure that their findings, on the whole, reflect the truth of what the aim of their study was.

Representativeness

- A sample of participants is selected to participate in the study (eg, a few A Level students). The purpose of a sample is that the findings from it reflect or 'represent' the group of people that the researcher is interested in (eg, all A Level students in the country), which is known as the target population. The aim of a sample is to allow the findings collected from a study to be representative (ie, typical) of the target population. Therefore, when we say the findings are 'representative' this means they reflect the views/behaviour of the target population. A study that is representative allows the researcher to make **generalisations** (draw conclusions) from it about the target population.

- If the study is not representative, it is not possible to make generalisations to the larger group in society (target population), which means the findings have no significance and limited use. The larger the sample of people used in the study, the greater the chance that the findings from study will be representative.

The relationship between validity and reliability

- The findings of research can be *reliable* but not *valid*. A study that consistently produces the same results when repeated does not necessarily reflect an accurate picture of what it ***set out*** to investigate. For example, a group of students used a questionnaire to investigate the drinking behaviour of their teachers on weekdays. The results showed that 1 out of 50 teachers said that they drank during the week. Is this likely to be a true reflection of their drinking behaviour? It is possible that the teachers lied on the questionnaire because they were afraid that the students would disapprove of their drinking habits. The students might administer the questionnaire on other occasions and the teachers might continue to lie, thus producing the same false results consistently. Such findings are *reliable,* but they lack validity because the study failed to find out about the teachers' real drinking habits.

Exam Questions

1. Outline **two** problems of using qualitative data in psychological research. . . . . **(4 marks)**

2. Outline **two** problems of using quantitative data in psychological research. . . . . **(4 marks)**

Measures of central Tendency and Dispersion

The AQA specification:

- Descriptive statistics: measures of central tendency – mean, median, mode; calculation of mean, median and mode; measures of dispersion; range and standard deviation; calculation of range

The exam requires that you are able to:

▶ Describe, identify and interpret the mean, mode and median.
▶ Give one advantage and one weakness of each type of measure of central tendency.
▶ Describe, identify and interpret the range and standard deviation.
▶ Give one advantage and one weakness for the range and standard deviation.

Introduction

We can summarise a large set of numbers from quantitative data in two ways. The first is by using a *measure of central tendency* that uses the *mean, median* and *mode* to tell us what the 'average' score is in a set of numbers.

The second way of summarising information is by using a *measure of dispersion* (range and standard deviation). This tells us how far the scores are spread away from the average score.

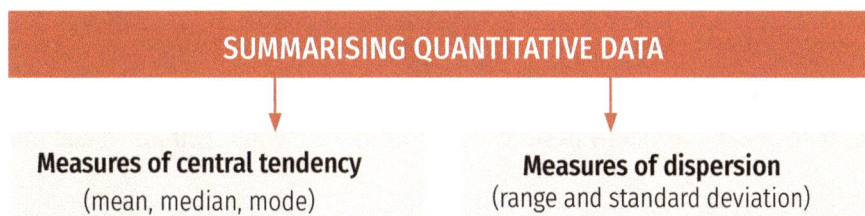

SUMMARISING QUANTITATIVE DATA

Measures of central tendency
(mean, median, mode)

Measures of dispersion
(range and standard deviation)

Measures of central tendency

There are three ways of measuring the average score in a given set of scores: these are the **mean, median** and **mode**. Together they are called **measures of central tendency** because they describe the midpoint in a set of numbers. You will need to use the most appropriate measure of central tendency to best sum up the data collected. Using the wrong one in your results may be misleading.

Mean

The **mean** is the most commonly used measure of central tendency. It is the 'average' value of all the scores. To find the mean value of a set of scores, add all the scores together and then divide by the *total number* of scores. The formula can be written like this:

$$\text{Mean} = \frac{\text{total sets of scores}}{\text{number of scores}}$$

FOR EXAMPLE:

Total sets of scores: 5, 8, 9, 3, 12, 16, 17,

$$\text{Mean} = \frac{5, 8, 9, 3, 12, 16, 17}{7}$$

Mean = 10

✓✗ Evaluation

✓ **Uses all data.**
It is the only measure of central tendency that uses all the scores in a set of data.

✗ **Prone to distortion.**
The average score can be skewed (distorted) by very high or low scores, which can give a misleading impression of the average score. These extreme scores are called outliers. For example, a set of scores obtained for the time taken to do a jigsaw puzzle activity was 5, 6, 5, 7, 5, 6 and 29 minutes. The mean score found for this distribution of scores was 9 minutes. But you can see that all the participants (apart from the extreme score of 29 minutes) completed the puzzle in 7 minutes or less, hence the average seems too high if we include the outlier!

Median

One way to overcome extreme scores in a set of data is to use another method called the **median**. The median is the *middle score* of a set of data. It is found by placing the scores in rank order of size, usually from the lowest to highest, and finding the middle number from the list.

FOR EXAMPLE:

Set of seven scores: 17, 5, 8, 9, 3, 12, 16

Arrange them in order, from lowest to highest: 3, 5, 8, 9, 12, 16, 17

Count to the middle value (fourth one along out of the seven here), which is 9.
MEDIAN = 9

Some sets of scores will have an even number of scores (the above example had an odd number), which means that there two scores rather than one in the middle position. To work out the median, you would add them together and divide by two.

FOR EXAMPLE:

Set of eight scores   19, 5, 8, 10, 3, 12, 16, 17

Arrange them in order, from lowest to highest: 3, 5, 8, 10, 12, 16, 17, 19

Count to the two middle values (fourth and fifth along out of the eight here), which are 10 and 12. Add them together and divide by two: 10+12 = 22 then 22÷2 = 11.
MEDIAN = 11

✓✗ Evaluation

✓ **Less affected by extreme scores.**
The median is not affected by outliers (extreme high and low scores). For example, in this set of thirteen scores, 2, 2, 3, 3, 3, 3, 4, 4, 5, 5, 5, 6, 47, the extreme outlier is 47. If we included it to calculate a mean, the mean is 7, which does not reflect the typical scores in this range set as 12 of them have a value of 6 or less. However, the median in this set is 4, which seems about right for this set of data.

✗ **Less accurate.**
The median is less accurate than the mean because it only looks at the two scores in the middle and does not use any of the other scores in the set. This is acceptable if the sets of scores are largely the same, but not when they are not. For example, in this set of nine scores, 2, 2, 2, 2, 15, 61, 69, 72, 75, the median is 15, which is not a good indication of the average set of scores. The mean would be approximately 33 in this case.

Mode

Mode refers to the most frequently occurring value (i.e. the most common) in a set of scores. If two values are most frequently occurring, this is called **bi-modal**. If three or more values are the most frequently occurring, this is called **multi-modal**. The mode can be used with any type of data, but it is the *only* measure of central tendency that can *only* be used for calculating *nominal* data.

FOR EXAMPLE:

Set of 11 scores: 2, 4, 4, 6, 6, 7, 7, 7, 10, 11, 12
Look for the most frequently occurring number, which is 7. This is the *mode value.*

Now take this set of 14 scores: 3, 3, 4, 5, 5, 5, 7, 7, 8, 8, 8, 11, 14, 15
There are two most frequently occurring numbers, 5 and 8. These are the *bi-modal values*.

✓✗ Evaluation

> ✓ **Less affected by extreme scores.**
>
> The mode – like the median – is not affected by extreme scores.

> ✗ **Less accurate.**
>
> The mode may not reflect the true average of a set of scores, especially if the most frequently occurring scores are either very high or very low. For example, in the set, 3, 3, 3, 34, 37, 42, 44, 50, 55, the mode is 3, however this does not accurately reflect the otherwise high set of scores.

Which measures to use

The advantages and disadvantages of using the mean, median and mode listed above should give you some indication of why and where you should use them.

Measures of central tendency	Most appropriate type of data	When to use it	Watch out
Mean	Mainly interval and ratio data	When there are no extreme scores (outliers)	The mean cannot be applied to nominal data.
Median	Mainly ordinal data	When there are extreme scores	The median cannot be applied to nominal data.
Mode	Mainly nominal data	When you want to know the frequency (how often something occurs)	Mode is the only one that can be applied to nominal data.

Measures of dispersion

Measures of central tendency may tell us about the average or midpoint score, but they do not   tell us much about the rest of the scores. For example, if we look at the table below, the mean scores for Class A and Class B are the same – namely 75 (Grade B). If we only describe the results using a measure of central tendency, it would suggest that both classes are both academically doing really well – when they are clearly not! The test scores for Class B are much more widely spread out than those of Class A. This is where a **measure of dispersion** is useful. It can tell us   of how widely the scores are dispersed (spread out) around the average score, or how close the other scores relate to the average score. This gives a better picture of the overall pattern in the set of data.

Class A test score	Class B test score
73 (grade B)	44 (grade E)
79 (grade B)	56 (grade D)
78 (grade B)	58 (grade D)
70 (grade B)	69 (grade C)
73 (grade B)	99 (grade A)
75 (grade B)	98 (grade A)
77 (grade B)	100 (grade A)
Mean = 75	**Mean = 75**
Average Grade B	Average Grade B

Finding the dispersion of scores can be done using the *range* and *standard deviation (SD)*. We will look at each one in turn.

Range

The **range** is the simplest way to work out a measure of dispersion (spread) of a set of scores. It is worked out by subtracting the lowest score from the highest score.

FOR EXAMPLE:

- In Class C, the highest test score is 61 and the lowest is 37. Take the lowest from the highest (61–37) to get the range = 24. Class D's scores are between 87 down to 3, so the range is (87–3) = 84. This shows that the spread of scores in Class B is much greater than that in Class A.

✓✗ Evaluation

> ✓ **Easy to calculate.**
> It is easy to calculate and see the range of scores at a glance.

> ✗ **Distorted by extreme scores.**
> The range can still be distorted by an extreme score, which will be misleading in terms of the real dispersion of scores. For example, in this set of scores – 4, 5, 7, 8, 9, 93 – the range would be 89, which is not a true picture of the scores because the lower scores are clustered together. One extreme score has widened the range disproportionately.

Standard deviation

The standard deviation (SD) is the most precise measure of dispersion. When working out the standard deviation, every score is involved in the calculation by taking the average distance of *each* score from the *mean*. The most important point for your exam is to appreciate what the size of the standard deviation means.

- A **small standard deviation** (number) means the scores are more alike and closer to the mean (average).

- A **big standard deviation** means the scores are quite different from each other and more spread out from the mean (average). See the table on the next page for an example.

Data Distributions

Once a set of data is collected and plotted on a histogram graph (with the y-axis representing the frequency and the x-axis representing the item of interest observed) this can display useful information and help us get a better understanding of what is going on. The 'shape' of the graph plotted tells us the how the scores were distributed. The overall pattern of the data is called a distribution. There are several types of data distributions. They are:

Normal Distributions

The most commonly referred to type of distribution is called a **normal distribution**. If you did this as a graph, it would be a curve that looked like a bell - a "bell curve". The "lump" at the top of the bell is where most of the scores bunch up, the flat ends to the left and the right are where the less common scores spread out. The defining features of a normal distribution are:

- the distribution is symmetrical around the **mid-point** and frequency of scores on the left side matches the distribution and frequency of scores on the right side.

- The **mean, median, and mode** of a normal distribution are identical and fall exactly in the centre of the curve – the mid-point.

- The dispersion of scores/measurements either side of the mid-point can be expressed in **standard deviation**.

Many human characteristics distributions fall on a normal curve. These normal distributions include height, weight, IQ, shoes size etc. This is important to understand because if a distribution is normal, there are certain qualities that are consistent and help in quickly understanding the scores within the distribution.

Interpreting normal distributions

If the mean is the 'lump' in the middle (mid-point), this means there are a bunch of scores that are close to the mean to the left and the right.

All the scores 34% lower or 34% higher than the mean (mid-point) - that's 68% of the total set of scores - are one Standard Deviation (1 SD) away from the mean. Being within 1 SD makes the score pretty "normal" statistically speaking. Therefore, any set of data that is normally distributed, 34.13% of the people will lie within one standard deviation below the mean and 34.13 will lie one standard deviation above the mean. Therefore, a total of 68.26% will lie within one standard deviation above or below the mean.

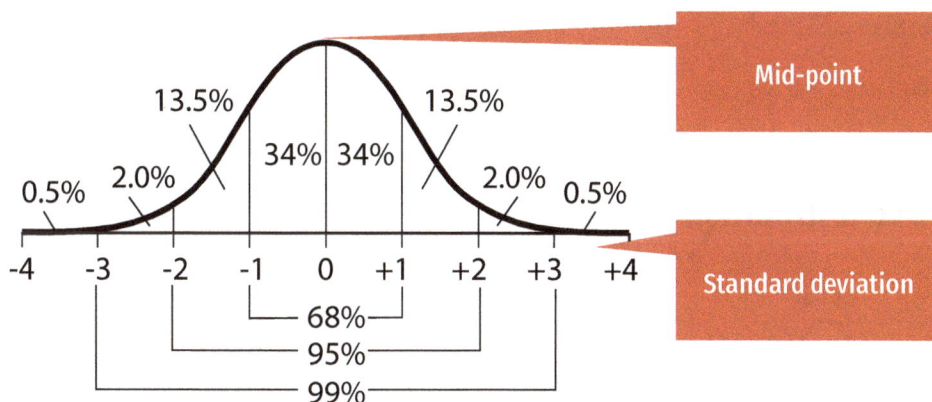

Two standard deviation (2 SD) means you add another 13.5% lower and 13.5% higher than that (68% + 24%) gives you 96% of all the scores who fall within 2 SD of the mean. Being within 2 SD makes you "unusual".

Then there are the people who fall outside the 96%, the ones in the bottom 2% and the top 2%. These scores are 3+ SD away from the mean and count as "very unusual".

As scores/values deviate further from the mean/median/mode they become less frequent giving the distribution a characteristic symmetrical bell shape. These extreme right and left scores from the midpoint are called 'tails' of the curve, which extend outwards but never, touches the x-axis.

Skewed Distributions

However, not all data will result in a perfect normal distribution. Some scores are not evenly distributed around the mean, this mean the scores this is a **skewed distribution**. The distribution of data is called skewed when it is not symmetrical at the mean (or median or mode) point; there is no even distribution scores either side of the mean. A skew can be positive or negative.

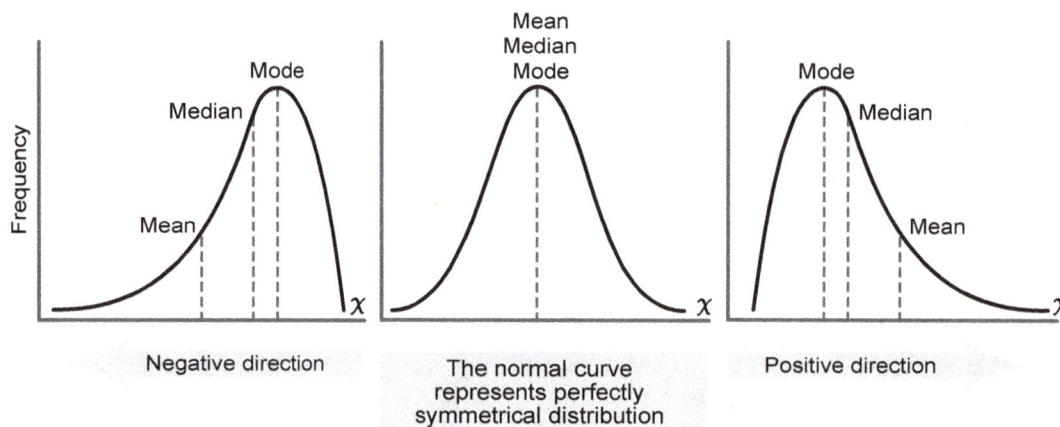

Negative direction | The normal curve represents perfectly symmetrical distribution | Positive direction

Positive Skewed distribution

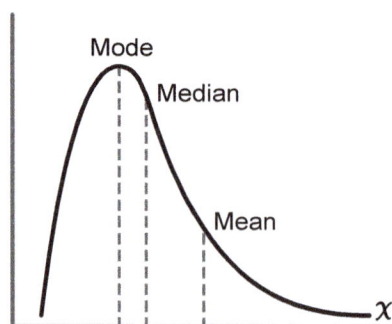

Positive direction

Positive skewered distribution is when most of the distribution is concentrated towards the left of the graph, which leave a long tail on the right (e.g. just a few people managed to acehive high scores).

Will contain more low than high score(s) –slightly lower mean than in a normal distribution

The measures of central tendency (mean, median and mode) will decrease in value

E.g. For example, many students getting low scores – the exam may have been too hard, with only a few getting high scores (fewer high extreme scores)

Negative skewed distribution

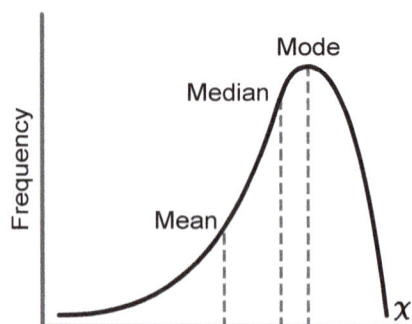

Negative direction

Negative skewered distribution the distribution is concentrated towards the right of the graph, which leave a long tail on the left (e.g. easy test with most of the scores remain on the right side of the graph)

Will contain more high than low score(s) –slightly higher mean than in a normal distribution

The measures of central tendency (mean, median and mode) will increase in value

E.g. For example, many students getting high scores – the exam may have been too easy, with only a few getting low scores (fewer low extreme scores)

The number of words were recalled by participants under condition 1 (after drinking a fizzy drink) and condition 2 (no fizzy drink).

An experiment to investigate the effect of fizzy drink has on memory recall

	With fizzy drink (condition 1)	Without fizzy drink (condition 2)
	27	58
	36	59
	60	60
	60	60
	84	61
	93	62
Mean	60	60
Standard deviation	25.81	1.41

The mean scores in both conditions in the table are the same – therefore we cannot tell whether drinking fizzy drinks or not drinking them improves memory recall. However, the standard deviation tells us a different story. The SD in condition 1 (with fizzy drinks) is larger than condition 2 (without fizzy drinks). This means that the memory recall task had a wider variation of scores from the participants in condition 1 than those in condition 2. We can conclude that some participants performed worse in the memory recall task after having a fizzy drink than those in condition 2.

✓✗ Evaluation

✓ **Sensitive.**
The SD is the most precise measure of dispersion because it uses the spread of all the scores.

✗ **Time consuming.**
Finding the SD is more time consuming and more difficult to calculate then the range.

1. A psychologist wanted to find out whether there is evidence that short-term memory fades with increasing age. To test this hypothesis, the researcher carried out a laboratory experiment. In group A, the people were aged between 20 and 40 years. In group B, their age ranged from 60 to 80 years. Both groups were required to learn a list of 20 words (nouns). Then, after a short period of time, they were asked to recall them. The table shows what the researcher found:

Participants	Condition A (20–40 years old) Number of nouns recalled correctly	Participant	Condition B (60–80 years old) Number of nouns recalled correctly
1	14	11	12
2	18	12	13
3	17	13	18
4	15	14	17
5	18	15	4
6	18	16	3
7	12	17	5
8	16	18	14
9	14	19	16
10	13	20	15
Measure of central tendency	15.5		11.7
Standard deviation	2.22		5.62

a) What measure of central tendency was used in the above data? . . . . **(1 mark)**

b) Explain one strength and one weakness of the measure of central tendency identified in question (a). . . . . **(2+2 marks)**

c) What does the standard deviation in this study tell us about the data? . . . . **(3 marks)**

2. The following scores were obtained in a memory test: 10, 15, 12, 15, 14, 13, 49, 11, 14, 12, 47.

a) Identify and explain which measure of central tendency that would be the most appropriate to use here. . . . . **(3 marks)**

3. Explain one strength and one weakness of the measure of central tendency identified in question 2. . . . . **(2+2 marks)**

The AQA specification:

- Presentation and display of quantitative data: graphs, tables, scattergrams, bar charts, histograms.

The exam requires that you are able to:

- ▶ Select the appropriate graphs, scattergrams or tables to illustrate quantitative data.
- ▶ Interpret and explain what graphs, scattergrams and tables indicate about the data..

Introduction

The information or results collected from a research study are referred to as *data* (or a data set). The form of the data can either be *quantitative* or *qualitative*. Here we concentrate on quantitative data.

Quantitative data

Research methods that tend to produce quantitative data are:

- **Experiments** (e.g. reaction-times in seconds to complete a task).
- **Structured observations** (e.g. tally scores on helping behaviour).
- **Self-report methods** (e.g. a 1–4 rating scale of anxiety levels).

Presentation and interpretation of quantitative data

Once a study has been completed, the researcher will have collected a lot of *raw data*. The next step is to *summarise* the data in a way that can easily be understood (analysed and interpreted). Quantitative data can be summarised and displayed using *descriptive statistics,* either numerically (e.g. mean, mode, and median) or visually (e.g. in a graph). They are called *descriptive* statistics because they *describe* the findings from the quantitative data.

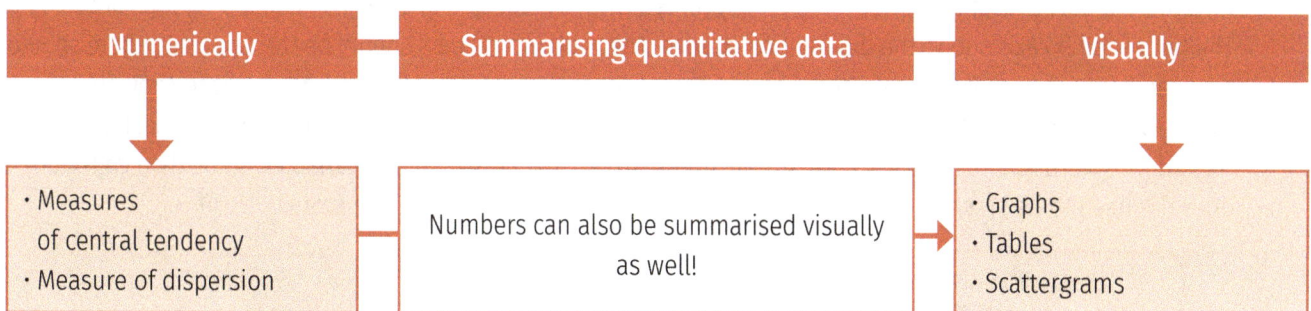

Numerically	Summarising quantitative data	Visually
• Measures of central tendency • Measure of dispersion	Numbers can also be summarised visually as well!	• Graphs • Tables • Scattergrams

Types of quantitative data

The type of data collected will determine the appropriate way to display the data (e.g. a bar chart or histogram) or which measure of central tendency to use (i.e. the mode, mean and median).The four different types of quantitative data that can be collected are nominal, ordinal, interval and ratio. They are known as **levels of measurements**.

- **Nominal data** – Nominal data involve recording results in *separate categories*. For example, a teacher may categorise which month each student was born (e.g. March or December). Each category is unrelated in as much as you can only be in one category (you can't be born in both March and December) so the data are also referred to as *non-continuous* data. There is no order of preference or rank of results, just separate categories.

- **Ordinal data** – The results are also recorded in separate categories, but this time the categories are *ranked in order* according to the results. For example, we can rank the winner and runners-up in a singing contest in terms of first (Elena), second (Maria), third (Natasha), and so on. However, ordinal data does not tell us the *difference* between each result (category), in as much as we do not know how much better the winner was than the runners-up. Ordinal data does not allow us to compare the results.

- **Interval data** – Like ordinal data, interval data is ranked in order, but this time the distances (or intervals) between each ranked order are *equal* to each other. For example, the number of days between the start of 1981 and 1982 is the same as those between 1983 and 1984 – namely 365 days. On a Fahrenheit temperature scale, the interval between 70 and 80 degrees is the same as that between 30 and 40 degrees – namely 10 degrees.

- **Ratio data** – This is the same as interval data, but for one difference – that is, ratio data have an absolute true *zero point*. The zero point allows comparisons to be made, such as 'twice as much' or 'half as much'. For example, if you ask three students how rich they are, student A may have £100, student B may have £50 and student C may have £25. So we can say that student A is twice as rich as student B, and four times as rich as student C. This is possible because the scale starts at zero, which signifies nothing (no money). You can see how this compares to interval data by looking at the Fahrenheit temperature example – 0 degrees does not mean *no* temperature at all – it is not a genuine zero but a *false* zero, just a point on a scale (because there are more temperatures below zero!).

Graphs, scattergrams and tables

Graphs and tables are excellent ways of displaying research findings in a clear way that can be understood. The type of graph you use will depend on the type of data collected (nominal, interval etc.). Care must be taken to choose the right graph to present the data. The wrong graph may present the data incorrectly or be visually misleading. For the exam, you will need to know the following about graphs, tables and scattergrams.

GRAPHS

Graphs include bar charts, histograms and frequency polygons (line graphs).

Bar charts

- **What are they used for?** They are used to display *nominal* or *ordinal* data in their various categories. They are also used to show all measures of central tendency (e.g. the mode, mean and median).

- **How are the data presented?** They are often presented with vertical bars to show individual or groups of scores. The horizontal (x) axis shows the different *categories*. The width of the bars should be the same and there should be a gap between each bar or category. The reason for not letting the bars touch each other is to show that the data is *noncontinuous*. That is, that there is no relationship between each category and thus the scores are not related. The vertical (y) axis shows the results (frequencies or amounts) of the variable. All the data collected does not need to be presented on the chart – only the most important or average scores.

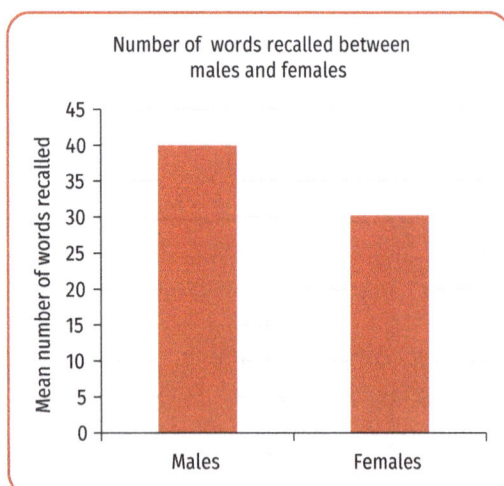

Number of words recalled between males and females

Bar charts ideal for	
Type of data:	Nominal, ordinal
Measures of central tendency:	Mean, mode, median

Histograms

- **What are they used for?** They are used to illustrate *interval* or *ratio* data (continuous data such as test scores 0–5, 6–10, 11–15, etc.).

- **How are the data presented?** The horizontal (x) axis is where you plot the *scores or values and* must be arranged in numerical order, usually from smallest to largest (e.g. 0–5 seconds, 6–10 seconds, 11–15 seconds). The vertical (y) axis shows the *frequencies,* that is, how many times something occurs. The bars must all be of equal width but – unlike in bar charts – they must have *no* gaps between the bars. This is to show that the data are continuous and are related.

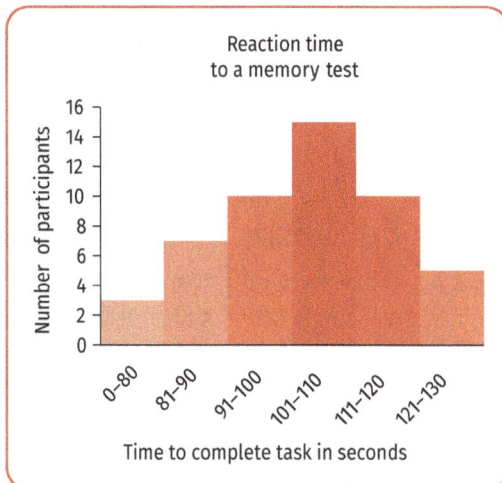

Reaction time to a memory test

Histogram ideal for	
Type of data :	Interval/ratio

Frequency polygons (line graphs)

- **What are they used for?** They are an alternative way of presenting the same information as histograms, (interval and ratio data), but are especially helpful for showing two sets of data at the same time, so that comparisons can be made.

- **How are the data presented?** The bars are replaced by lines. The lines connect the *midpoints* of the tops of the bars (as they would appear in a histogram) and when they are joined they form a line.

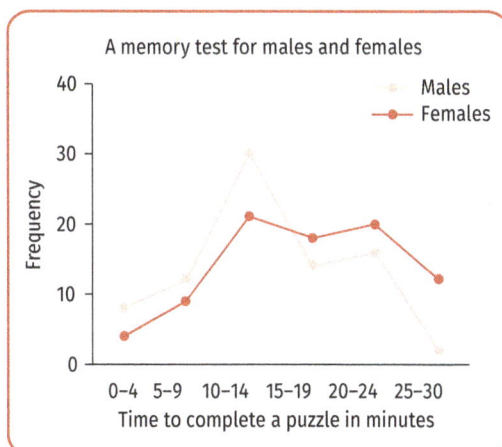

A memory test for males and females

Frequency polygon ideal	
Type of data:	Interval/ratio

Tables

- **What are they used for?** Tables are used to summarise the research findings of average scores (e.g. medians, means and modes) and to display the range and standard deviation (SD) of scores.

- **How are the data presented?** Data are arranged in tables and columns. There must be a clear title above the table, and each row and column in the table will also need to be clearly labelled.

Memory tests on students at different times of the day

	Memory test scores for students in the morning	Memory test scores for students in the afternoon
Mean score	23	39
Standard deviation	1.7	3.2

Scattergrams

- **What are they used for?** Scattergrams are also known as scattergraphs or scatterplots. They are used to present research findings that produce **correlational** data. They are plots of the scores of a person or phenomenon under conditions of two different variables, and will show any relationship that exists between them (e.g. poverty and exam results or stress and heart disease).

- **How are the data presented?** The data from one of the variables is placed on the horizontal (x) axis and the data from the other variable is placed on the vertical (y) axis. It does not matter which variable goes on which axis. Where the two scores intersect (meet) on the graph, a mark is plotted. Once all the scores have been placed there will be a scattering of dots on the graph, where each dot represents a single score. A best-fit line can be drawn between these scattered points. Correlational data shows the type of relationship between the two variables as either positive or negative – or no relationship at all. The following scattergrams show the different types of relationship between drinking beer and exam performance.

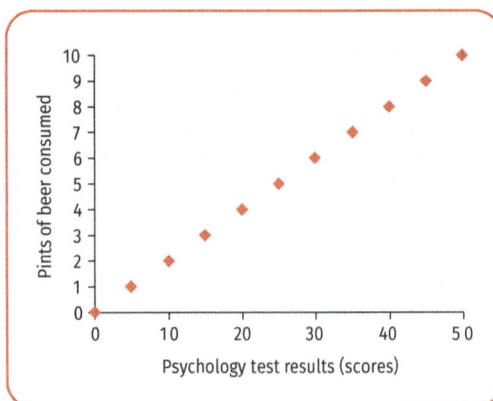

Perfect positive correlation

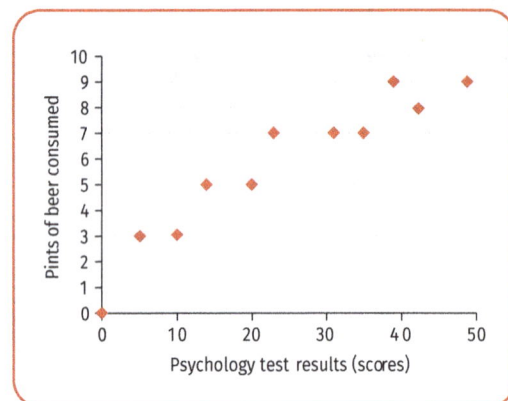

Strong positive correlation

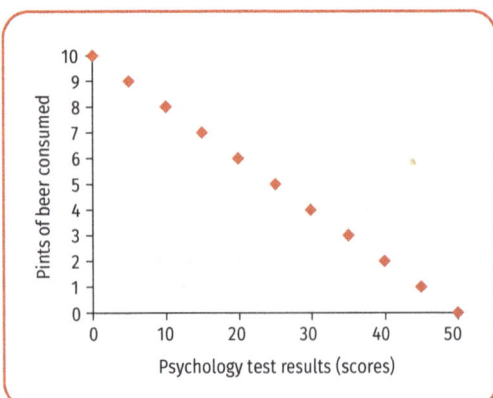

Perfect negative correlation

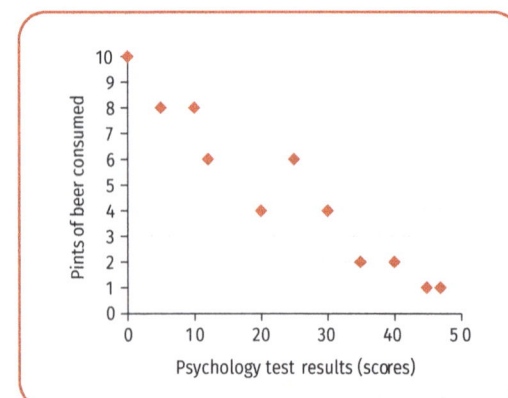

Strong negative correlation

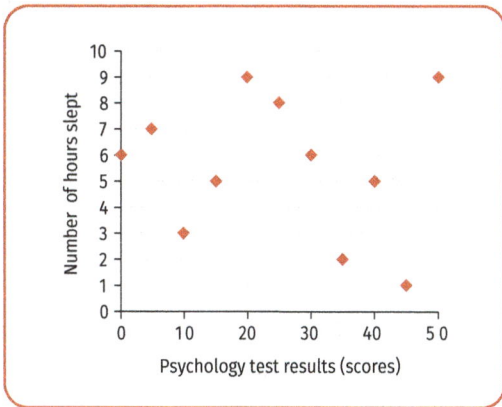

Number of hours slept / Psychology test results (scores)

No correlation

Scattergrams ideal for	
Type of data:	ordinal/interval/ratio

Exam Questions

1. A psychology teacher, Mr Twirl, was curious to see whether there was a correlation between the time spent on Facebook and exam performance among students. Below are Mr Twirl's findings from 20 students in his AS Level psychology class.

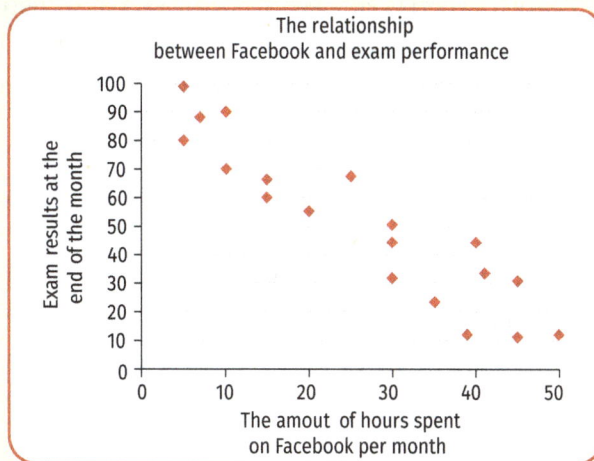

The relationship between Facebook and exam performance

Exam results at the end of the month / The amout of hours spent on Facebook per month

a) Using the scattergram, describe the relationship between Facebook usage and exam performance. . . . . **(2 marks)**

b) Identify the two variables in this study. . . . . **(1+ 1 marks)**

c) Explain one difficulty in drawing a conclusion from this data. . . . . **(2 marks)**

The AQA specification:

- Introduction to statistical testing; the sign test.

The exam requires that you are able to:

▶ Understand the terms 'probability' and 'significance' and how this is applied in psychological research to calculate the statistical significance of quantitative research data.
▶ Understand the factors that affect the choice of statistical tests to analyse a set of data.
▶ Understand how to use the 'sign test'.

Key terms

- **Probability:** calculates the likelihood that an event will happen a on a numerical scale from 0 to 1 (0 indicating never and 1 indicating certainty).

- **Significance:** in inferential statistics, significance refers to the view that the results obtained from a study were very unlikely to have occurred by chance.

- **Inferential statistics:** refers to a statistical test that is used to analyse a set of data to determine the probability that the results occurred by chance. The results are viewed as significant (hypothesis accepted) if the mathematical probability demonstrates the likelihood of this occurring by chance was very small. This allows us to infer or draw a conclusion from the sample taken, enabling us to generalise the findings to the wider population.

Introduction

There are two types of statistics that are used to analyse quantitative data. There are descriptive **statistics,** which involve *summarising* quantitative data using charts, graphs and tables as a measure of central tendency, allowing the researcher to understand and describe the findings from the data. However, descriptive data cannot explain how important the results are. To determine how significant the results really are, the researcher will then need to apply a test called **inferential statistics**. Before we begin to understand statistical tests we need to understand the concepts of *probability* and *significance* so we get a clearer picture of how these are applied to inferential statistics.

Probability

Probability (symbol *p*) calculates the likelihood that an event will happen. This is expressed as a numerical number on a scale of 1 and 0 (which can be converted to a fraction or percentage). An event with a probability of 1 means it is certain to happen (100%). e.g. the probability of a coin being tossed and resulting in either 'heads' or 'tails' is 1, because there are no other options. The probability of 0 means it is impossible for it to happen. For example, the probability that the coin will land without either side facing up is 0 (if it lands flat), because either 'heads' or 'tails' must be facing up. An event with a probability of 0.5 (50%) means there is equal chance of something occurring or not occurring. E.g. the probability of getting 'heads' if you toss a coin is 1 in 2 and is written as p = 0.5 (50%), because the toss is equally likely to result in 'tails'. The nearer the number is to 1 the greater the chance of it occurring; the closer to 0, the more unlikely it is to occur. Take, for example, a bag that contains 10 blue and 2 green marbles. The probability of pulling out a blue marble will be 0.8 (80 %) and a green marble 0.2 (20%).

The formula for probability:

$$\text{Possibility of event} = \frac{\text{The number of successful outcomes}}{\text{Total number of possible outcomes}}$$

- To convert a probability from a decimal to a percentage, multiple the decimal by 100. For example, 0.25 x 100 = 25%
- To convert a probability from a percentage to a decimal, divide the percentage by 100. For example, 30% =0.30.

Let's take the example of someone trying to find out the probability of rolling a four on a six-sided die. Rolling a four would be the 'number of successful outcomes', (which is one) and since we know that a six-sided die can land any one of six numbers, the 'total number of possible outcomes' is six. We write P(heads) = ⅙ (16.67%)

Significance

Statistical tests allow us to know how significant or non-significant the results from a study are. The term **significance** means that the probability that the results occurred by chance/error is very small. This will tell us whether the research hypothesis is true (relationship exists between the variables) or the null hypothesis is true (no relationship exist between the variables). In order to understand significance a little more, let's take the following hypothesis that:

- **Eating garlic has an effect on memory recall in short-term memory**
- **Eating garlic has no effect on memory recall in short-term memory**

If the results are:
Significant: the null hypothesis is rejected and the research hypothesis is accepted, as the test shows a very low possibility that the findings occurred by chance **(i.e. garlic improves memory recall in STM)**.

Not significant: the null hypothesis is accepted, and the research hypothesis is rejected, as there is a probability that the results occurred by chance. Therefore there is no relationship or difference between the variables of what you were trying to discover **(i.e. garlic has no effect on memory recall in STM)**.

Level(s) of significance

Once the results have been calculated, a level of probability is chosen using a statistical test; usually it will be either at '0.05' (5%) or '0.01' (1%) level. In psychology the generally agreed level, 5%, is often written as **P=≤0.05** or **P= 5%**. The level of probability (*p* value) chosen will determine if the null hypothesis can be rejected in favour of the research hypothesis.

- The expression $p ≤ 0.05$ refers to the probability that the results occurring through chance is less than or equal to 0.05. In other words, there is 5% (1 in 20) risk that the results occurred by chance. To put it another way, if you did the experiment 100 times, the pattern of results occurring by chance is less than 5 times in 100. This means that we can be 95% certain that the results did not happen by chance and therefore we can conclude the results are significant, showing a relationship between the variables.

- If the statistical test shows that the results had a probability which is higher than 5% we can conclude that the findings are not that significant and were probably due to chance factors. In a nutshell:

  - **Hypothesis is accepted when $p ≤ 0.05$ (significant)**
  - **Null hypothesis is accepted when $p ≥ 0.05$ (not significant)**

As a rule of thumb

As rule of thumb, the smaller the p value, the more significant the results are. The higher the p value, the less significant they become. However, it is important to note that sometimes probability level in psychological research is set at **$p ≤ 0.01$**. This is a much stricter level which means there is a 99% that the results did not occur by chance, giving us greater confidence in the results. This is usually for research where there are health or social implications that can be sensitive or damaging (e.g. drug testing) to avoid taking any chances!

Examples of level of probability

P values	As a percentage	Explanation
P = 0.5	50%	1 in 2 probability results caused by chance
P = 0.1	10%	1 in 10 probability results caused by chance
P = 0.05	5%	1 in 20 probability results caused by chance
P = 0.01	1%	1 in 100 probability results caused by chance

Statistical tests

There are different types of statistics tests that are used to determine whether the results obtained from the research are significant or not. They are:

- Sign test
- Spearman's Rho test
- Mann-Whitney U test
- Wilcoxon T test
- Chi-squared test
- Pearson's r,
- related t-test,
- unrelated t-test

Observed values and critical values

Once you have selected the appropriate statistical tests (will come to that shortly), this will require some calculation on your data which will eventually produce a number (in all statistical tests) called the **observed value** (e.g. $T = 4.45$ or $rho = +0.78$). For each of the four statistical tests the observed values are given different names. For example:

Name of statistical test	The name of the observed value
Sign test	S
Spearman's correlation	rho
Mann–Whitney U	U
Wilcoxon	T
Chi-squared	X^2
Pearson's r,	r
related t-test	t
unrelated t-test	t

To see if the observed value is significant, the number (e.g. $rho = +0.78$) is then compared to another number which can be found in a statistical table called the **table of critical values** (or just **critical values**). In some statistical tests, for the result to be significant:

- The observed value must be **equal to or larger** than the critical value for the null hypothesis to be rejected.

For other statistical tests:

- The observed value must be **equal or smaller** than the critical value for the null hypothesis to be rejected.

How to remember

If there is an 'R' in the name of the statistical test (e.g. Spearman and chi-squared) than the observed value should be gReateR than the critical value. If there is no R in the name of the test (e.g. Mann-Whitney and Wilcoxon) then the observed value should be less than the critical value.

Level of significance for two tailed test			
0.10	0.05	0.02	0.01
Level of significance for one tailed test			
0.05	0.025	0.01	0.005
N =			
4	1.000		
5	0.900	1.000	1.000
6	0.829	0.886	0.943	1.000
7	0.714	0.786	0.893	0.929
8	0.643	0.738	0.833	0.881
9	0.600	0.700	0.783	0.883
10	0.564	0.648	0.745	0.794
11	0.536	0.618	0.709	0.755
12	0.503	0.587	0.671	0.727
13	0.484	0.560	0.648	0.703
14	0.464	0.538	0.622	0.675
15	0.443	0.521	0.604	0.654
16	0.429	0.503	0.582	0.635
17	0.414	0.485	0.566	0.615
18	0.401	0.472	0.550	0.600
19	0.391	0.460	0.535	0.584
20	0.380	0.447	0.520	0.570
21	0.370	0.435	0.508	0.556
22	0.361	0.425	0.496	0.544
23	0.353	0.415	0.486	0.532
24	0.344	0.406	0.476	0.521
25	0.337	0.398	0.466	0.511
26	0.331	0.390	0.457	0.501
27	0.324	0.382	0.448	0.491
28	0.317	0.375	0.440	0.483
29	0.312	0.368	0.433	0.475
30	0.306	0.362	0.425	0.467

Example of a critical value of Spearman's correlation

In this case, the observed value of *rho* must be equal to or larger than the critical values in the table for the result to be significant (reject the null hypothesis).

At this level of significance, there is a probability of 5% that the results were due to chance/error.

N = number of participants

These numbers are the critical values.

Factors affecting choice of statistical test

How to choose the correct statistical test? The choice of statistical test will depend on three main factors:

- **Research hypothesis** (are you testing for a difference or a correlation?)
- **Levels of measurement** (what type of data is it: nominal, ordinal, interval?)
- **Is the data related or unrelated?** (are the same participants or different participants being used?)

Research hypothesis

What is the research hypothesis trying to show? Is it looking for a *difference* in the sample of data collected from the two conditions? For example, in the hypothesis 'young males have more car accidents then young females', you are predicting a difference in driving between the two groups (teenage male and female drivers). Or is the research looking for a *correlation* (relationship) between a set of scores? For example, 'the older you get the more car accidents you have' (this is predicting a relationship between age and accidents).

Levels of measurement

The type of data collected in the study will determine the appropriate statistical test to use. The four different types of quantitative data that can be collected are nominal, ordinal, interval and ratio. They are known as **levels of measurements**.

- **Nominal data** involves recording results in *separate categories*. For example, a teacher may categorise which month each student was born (e.g. March or December). Each category is unrelated in as much as you can only be in one category (you can't be born in both March and December) so the data is also referred to as *non-continuous* data. There is no order of preference or rank of results, just separate categories.

- **Ordinal data** involves reordering the data in separate categories, but this time the categories are *ranked in order* according to the results. For example, we can rank the winner and runners-up in a singing contest in terms of first (Elena), second (Maria), third (Natasha), and so on. However, ordinal data does not tell us the *difference* between each result (category), in as much as we do not know how much better the winner was than the runners-up. Ordinal data does not allow us to compare the results.

- **Interval data,** like ordinal data, is ranked in order, but this time the distances (or intervals) between the ranked orders are *equal* to each other. For example, the number of days between the start of 1981 and 1982 is the same as those between 1983 and 1984 – namely 365 days. On a Fahrenheit temperature scale, the interval between 70 and 80 degrees is the same as that between 30 and 40 degrees – namely 10 degrees.

- **Ratio data** is the same as interval data, but for one difference – ratio data has an absolute true *zero point*. The zero point allows comparisons to be made, such as 'twice as much' or 'half as much'. For example, if you ask three students how rich they are, student A may have £100, student B may have £50 and student C may have £25. So we can say that student A is twice as rich as student B, and four times as rich as student C. This is possible because the scale starts at zero, which signifies nothing (no money). You can see how this compares to interval data by looking at the Fahrenheit temperature example – 0 degrees does not mean *no* temperature at all. It is not a genuine zero but a *false* zero, just a point on a scale (because there are more temperatures below zero!).

Related and unrelated data

Next you will need to see if you have related or unrelated data:

- **Unrelated data (independent measures):** the participants were used in only one condition (i.e. different participants were used for different conditions, never in two conditions). Each participant produces only one set of data which is usually then compared with another person's data.

- **Related data (repeated measures):** the same participants are used in all the conditions. This is so you can compare the score of each participant in one condition with their own performance in the other condition.

How to use the critical values table

To find the appropriate critical value in a table you will need to know:

- **Number of participants.** For the Spearman's Rho, Wilcoxon and Mann Whitney U you need to know the number of participants used in the group(s) study, which is written as 'N'. In studies using *independent group design* there are two values for N (one for each group of participants) called N1 and N2. For the Chi-squared test, you will also need to know the degree of freedom (df). This is calculated by the number of cells there are (number of rows in your table – 1) (number of columns in your table – 1). For example, if your table has 4 rows and 2 columns, the calculation for the df = (4-1)(2-1) =3. For a two by two table (two columns and two rows) df is 1 and for a three by two table df is 2.

- o **One tailed or two tailed test.** If the research hypothesis was a directional hypothesis, then you use a one tailed test, if it was a non-directional you use a two tailed test.
- o **Significance level.** What is the stated level of significance selected? (E.g. $p \leq 0.05$)

The sign test

To determine whether the results are significant, we can use a statistical test called the **sign test**. There are different types of statistics tests that are used to determine whether the results, but this will depend on the conditions/design of your research methods. To use the sign test, you will need to ensure that:

- **Difference:** when you are looking for a difference between two sets of data.

- **Repeated measures design:** requires two sets of scores from the same person so it can be compared to see if there is a difference (e.g. repeated measures or from matched pairs).

- **Nominal data:** when the data collected falls into classified category (e.g. Attachment A, B, C, D) and the data is in frequencies (e.g. using a tally system) rather than in scores.

How to use THE SIGN TEST?

When to use the Sign test...

- o Association/Difference: when you are looking for a difference between two sets of data.
- o Related data: requires two sets of scores from the same person so it can be compared to see if there is a difference (e.g. repeated measures or from matched pairs).
- o Nominal data: when the data collected falls into classified category (Attachment A, B, C, D) and the data is in frequencies (e.g. using a tally system) rather than in scores.

How to use the sign test...

Step 1 →	Step 2 →	Step 3 →	Step 4 →	Step 5 →	Step 6
• State the alternative hypothesis and whether it is directional/non-directional. • Identity the null hypothesis.	• Draw a contingency table. • Calculate the total of observed frequency for each row and column of the table and the grand total.	• Find the expected frequency.	• Find the observed value of S.	• Find the table's critical value of S.	• State the conclusion of what the study found, by determining if the results are significant or not.

STEP 1: State the alternative and null hypothesis

We will use a hypothetical study to show you how to use the sign test.

A psychologist is interested in the effects that therapy has on a person's level of depression. She asks participants to rate their level of depression by giving a score out of 100 on two occasions: before they start treatment and again after five treatment sessions. The higher the score the more depressed they feel. The results are shown below:

Participants	Depressed rating before treatment Condition A	Depressed rating after five treatment sessions Condition B
1	63	58
2	85	22
3	60	33
4	75	78
5	95	75
6	60	60
7	85	46
8	80	55
9	90	65
10	78	72

The study will investigate whether having therapy can reduce depression. Therefore the hypothesis will be:

- **Alternative hypothesis:** Therapy will reduce the levels of depression experienced by people.

- **Null hypothesis:** Therapy will have no effect on the levels of depression experienced by people.

> ✓ **NOTE:**
> The sign test cannot be used when there are fewer than six scores.

> ✓ **NOTE:**
> As previous research suggests that therapy is effective, a one-tailed hypothesis is chosen.

Once you (or the researcher) has gathered his or her data, the test statistics for the sign test can be calculated as follows:

STEP 2: Draw a table to show the difference

1. Draw up table

The first job is to take the raw data to be analysed and place it into table format. You will need four columns (going from left to right): Number of participants; Condition 1; Condition 2; Direction of difference. An example of a table is provided below, which represents the data obtained from our therapy study.

Give each pair of scores a plus or minus sign

Next, for each participant's pair of scores, give a plus (+) if the score in column B is greater than the score in column A, give a minus (−) if the score in column B is lower than the score in column A, and give a zero (0) if the scores are the same. An example has already been done for you:

Participants	Depressed rating before treatment Condition A	Depressed rating after five treatment sessions Condition B	Direction of difference (B-A)
1	63	58	− (decrease)
2	85	22	− (decrease)

3	60	33	– (decrease)
4	75	78	+ (increase)
5	95	75	– (decrease)
6	60	60	0 (no change)
7	85	46	– (decrease)
8	80	55	– (decrease)
9	90	65	– (decrease)
10	78	72	– (decrease)

STEP 3: Find the observed value for S

Next, you need to add up how many of the less frequent sign there are, and call this 'S'. Ignore all the zeros. In the table above, the plus sign occurs less frequently (only once) than the minus sign, therefore S =1

STEP 4: Find the table's critical value of S

Before you look at the table's critical values for the sign test, you will need to know the following information:

Number of participants: Count the number of participants (N) whose scores have changed in either direction (ignore the zeros i.e. scores that remained the same). In the table above, one participant's score remained the same therefore, N=9

Type of hypothesis
Identify the type of hypothesis for your study: directional hypothesis (one-tailed test) or a non-directional hypothesis (two-tailed test). In our example, we have chosen a one-tailed hypothesis.

Your chosen level of significance
The level of significance you could select for your study is usually $p \leq 0.05$ or $p \leq 0.01$. In our study we will assume $p = \leq 0.05$.

Now use the table to compare the table's critical value to your observed value
Now look at the tables of critical values for the sign test; identify your chosen significance level and the type of hypothesis selected (one-tailed test or two-tailed test hypothesis). Now, look down the left hand column (N) until you reach the appropriate number of participants (which in our case, N = 9), then look across the row for N=9 to find the critical value for S. Compare this with your observed value of *S*. The calculated value for S must be equal to or less than the critical value for the difference to be significant. If S is greater than the critical value the results are not significant.

> ✓ **For the sign test**
> the observed value (S) must be equal or less than the critical value to be accepted as significant, allowing the null hypothesis to be rejected.

STEP 6: State the conclusion

As the observed value (1) for a one-tailed hypothesis at $p \leq 0.05$ and N = 9, is equal to the critical value (1), we can reject the null hypothesis and accept the alternative hypothesis that therapy does have a positive effect on people's level of depression.

Table of Critical Values for Sign test

N	One-tailed		Two-tailed	
	0.05	0.1	0.05	0.01
1	-	-	-	-
2	-	-	-	-
3	-	-	-	-
4	-	-	-	-
5	0	-	-	-
6	0	-	0	-
7	0	0	0	-
8	1	0	0	0
9	1	0	1	0
10	1	0	1	0
11	2	0	1	0
12	2	1	2	1
13	3	1	2	1
14	3	1	2	1
15	3	2	3	2
16	4	2	3	2
17	4	2	4	2
18	5	3	4	3
19	5	3	4	3
20	5	3	5	3
21	6	4	5	4
22	6	4	5	4
23	7	4	6	4
24	7	5	6	5
25	7	5	7	5
26	8	6	7	6
27	8	6	7	6
28	9	6	8	6
29	9	7	8	7
30	10	7	9	7
31	10	7	9	7
32	10	8	9	8
33	11	8	10	8
34	11	9	10	9
35	12	9	11	9
36	12	9	11	9
37	13	10	12	10
38	13	10	12	10
39	13	11	12	11
40	14	11	13	11

The calculated value of the Sign test must be equal to or larger than the critical value (number shown in in the table), which means the hypothesis is accepted and the null hypothesis can be rejected.

The AQA specification:

A-LEVEL ONLY

- Probability and significance: use of statistical tables and critical values in interpretation of significance; Type I and Type II errors.

The exam requires that you are able to:

▶ Understand the terms 'probability' and 'significance' and how this is applied in psychological research to calculate the statistical significance of quantitative research data.

▶ Understand how Type 1 and Type 2 errors can arise and how they can affect the interpretation of the results of statistical analysis.

▶ Understand the factors that affect the choice of statistical tests to analyse a set of data.

▶ Analyse and interpret data to see whether it is statistically significant or not.

Key terms

- **Probability:** calculates the likelihood that an event will happen a on a numerical scale from 0 to 1 (0 indicating never and 1 indicating certainty).

- **Significance:** in inferential statistics, significance refers to the view that the results obtained from a study were very unlikely to have occurred by chance.

- **Type 1 error:** this type of error occurs when the statistical analysis of the data demonstrates the null hypothesis should be rejected, but it is in fact actually true.

- **Type 2 error:** this type of error occurs when the statistical analysis of the data demonstrates that the null hypothesis it accepted as being true was in fact false and should be rejected.

- **Inferential statistics:** refers to a statistical test that is used to analyse a set of data to determine the probability that the results occurred by chance. The results are viewed as significant (hypothesis accepted) if the mathematical probability demonstrates the likelihood of this occurring by chance was very small. This allows us to infer or draw a conclusion from the sample taken, enabling us to generalise the findings to the wider population.

Introduction

There are two types of statistics that are used to analyse quantitative data. There are descriptive **statistics,** which involve *summarising* quantitative data using charts, graphs and tables as a measure of central tendency, allowing the researcher to understand and describe the findings from the data. However, descriptive data cannot explain how important the results are. To determine how significant the results really are, the researcher will then need to apply a test called **inferential statistics**. Before we begin to understand statistical tests we need to understand the concepts of *probability* and *significance* so we get a clearer picture of how these are applied to inferential statistics.

Probability

Probability (symbol *p*) calculates the likelihood that an event will happen. This is expressed as a numerical number on a scale of 1 and 0 (which can be converted to a fraction or percentage). An event with a probability of 1 means it is certain to happen (100%). e.g. the probability of a coin being tossed and resulting in either 'heads' or 'tails' is 1, because there are no other options. The probability of 0 means it is impossible for it to happen. For example, the probability that the coin will land without either side facing up is 0 (if it lands flat), because either 'heads' or 'tails' must be facing up.

An event with a probability of 0.5 (50%) means there is equal chance of something occurring or not occurring. E.g. the probability of getting 'heads' if you toss a coin is 1 in 2 and is written as p = 0.5 (50%), because the toss is equally likely to result in 'tails'. The nearer the number is to 1 the greater the chance of it occurring; the closer to 0, the more unlikely it is to occur. Take, for example, a bag that contains 10 blue and 2 green marbles. The probability of pulling out a blue marble will be 0.8 (80 %) and a green marble 0.2 (20%).

The formula for probability:

$$\text{Possibility of event} = \frac{\text{The number of successful outcomes}}{\text{Total number of possible outcomes}}$$

- ○ To convert a probability from a decimal to a percentage, multiple the decimal by 100. For example, 0.25 x 100 = 25%
- ○ To convert a probability from a percentage to a decimal, divide the percentage by 100. For example, 30% =0.30.

Let's take the example of someone trying to find out the probability of rolling a four on a six-sided die. Rolling a four would be the 'number of successful outcomes', (which is one) and since we know that a six-sided die can land any one of six numbers, the 'total number of possible outcomes' is six. We write P(heads) = ⅙ (16.67%)

Significance

Statistical tests allow us to know how significant or non-significant the results from a study are. The term **significance** means that the probability that the results occurred by chance/error is very small. This will tell us whether the research hypothesis is true (relationship exists between the variables) or the null hypothesis is true (no relationship exist between the variables). In order to understand significance a little more, let's take the following hypothesis that:

- ○ Eating garlic has an effect on memory recall in short-term memory
- ○ Eating garlic has no effect on memory recall in short-term memory

If the results are:

Significant: the null hypothesis is rejected and the research hypothesis is accepted, as the test shows a very low possibility that the findings occurred by chance **(i.e. garlic improves memory recall in STM)**.

Not significant: the null hypothesis is accepted, and the research hypothesis is rejected, as there is a probability that the results occurred by chance. Therefore there is no relationship or difference between the variables of what you were trying to discover **(i.e. garlic has no effect on memory recall in STM)**.

Level(s) of significance

Once the results have been calculated, a level of probability is chosen using a statistical test; usually it will be either at '0.05' (5%) or '0.01' (1%) level. In psychology the generally agreed level, 5%, is often written as **P=≤0.05** or **P= 5%**. The level of probability (*p* value) chosen will determine if the null hypothesis can be rejected in favour of the research hypothesis.

- • The expression p ≤ 0.05 refers to the probability that the results occurring through chance is less than or equal to 0.05. In other words, there is 5% (1 in 20) risk that the results occurred by chance. To put it another way, if you did the experiment 100 times, the pattern of results occurring by chance is less than 5 times in 100. This means that we can be 95% certain that the results did not happen by chance and therefore we can conclude the results are significant, showing a relationship between the variables.

- If the statistical test shows that the results had a probability which is higher than 5% we can conclude that the findings are not that significant and were probably due to chance factors. In a nutshell:
  - **Hypothesis is accepted when p ≤ 0.05 (significant)**
  - **Null hypothesis is accepted when p ≥ 0.05 (not significant)**

As a rule of thumb
As rule of thumb, the smaller the p value, the more significant the results are. The higher the p value, the less significant they become. However, it is important to note that sometimes probability level in psychological research is set at **p ≤ 0.01.** This is a much stricter level which means there is a 99% that the results did not occur by chance, giving us greater confidence in the results. This is usually for research where there are health or social implications that can be sensitive or damaging (e.g. drug testing) to avoid taking any chances!

Examples of level of probability

P values	As a percentage	Explanation
P = 0.5	50%	1 in 2 probability results caused by chance
P = 0.1	10%	1 in 10 probability results caused by chance
P = 0.05	5%	1 in 20 probability results caused by chance
P = 0.01	1%	1 in 100 probability results caused by chance

Type 1 and Type 2 error
Statistical tests calculate the probability, never the certainty of the results; there is always a possibility the findings were not significant and they occurred by chance. Sometimes the results of statistical tests produce an incorrect decision as to whether to accept or reject the null hypothesis. Possible mistakes based on the results from a statistical test are called **Type 1 error** and **Type 2 error**.

- **Type I error** (known as false positive error): this occurs when the null hypothesis is rejected when really it was correct. This can happen even though the statistical test found significant support for the research hypothesis. If this is the case, we have made a Type 1 error. The likelihood of making a Type 1 error is 5% at p ≤ 0.05 and 1% at p ≤ 0.01; therefore it is more likely to occur when p ≤ 0.05, as there is a larger margin of error which can lead to wrongly accepting the research hypothesis. When the level of significance is set at 5%, there will always be a one in twenty chance or less that the results are due to chance factors rather than to the influence of the independent variable.

- **Type 2 error** (known as false negative error): occurs when the null hypothesis is accepted when really it was wrong to do so. If the statistical test found that the results were not significant when they really were, we have made a Type 2 error. This is more likely to occur when the level of significance is set at p ≤ 0.01 (1%), as there is a 1 in 100 chance or less that the results were really due to the independent variable rather than chance factors. This is because the margin of error is small, which makes it harder to accept the research hypothesis at p ≤ 0.01 than it is at p ≤ 0.05.

Garlic improves memory	Garlic does improve memory
Type 1 error **Accepting the hypothesis when the null hypothesis is true**	Correction decision should have been... **Do not reject the null hypothesis as it is in fact true**
Type 2 error **Accepting the null hypothesis when the research hypothesis is true**	Correction decision should have been... **Reject the null hypothesis as it is in fact false**

Compromise

Choosing a significance level is a compromise; if we set the significance level to very strict, such as $p \leq 0.01$, then we lower the chances of making a Type 1 error but increase the risk of making Type 2 error. If we set the significance level at $p \leq 0.05$ then you increase the risk of making a Type 1 error.

Statistical tests

There are different types of statistics tests that are used to determine whether the results obtained from the research are significant or not. They are:

- Sign test
- Spearman's Rho test
- Mann-Whitney U test
- Wilcoxon T test
- Chi-squared test
- Pearson's r,
- related t-test,
- unrelated t-test

Observed values and critical values

Once you have selected the appropriate statistical tests (will come to that shortly), this will require some calculation on your data which will eventually produce a number (in all statistical tests) called the **observed value** (e.g. $T = 4.45$ or $rho = +0.78$). For each of the four statistical tests the observed values are given different names. For example:

Name of statistical test	The name of the observed value
Sign test	S
Spearman's correlation	rho
Mann–Whitney U	U
Wilcoxon	T
Chi-squared	X^2
Pearson's r,	r
related t-test	t
unrelated t-test	t

To see if the observed value is significant, the number (e.g. $rho = +0.78$) is then compared to another number which can be found in a statistical table called the **table of critical values** (or just **critical values**). In some statistical tests, for the result to be significant:

- The observed value must be **equal to or larger** than the critical value for the null hypothesis to be rejected.

For other statistical tests:

- The observed value must be **equal or smaller** than the critical value for the null hypothesis to be rejected.

How to remember

One way to remember...
If there is an 'R' in the name of the statistical test (e.g. Spearman and chi-squared) than the observed value should be gReateR than the critical value. If there is no R in the name of the test (e.g. Mann-Whitney and Wilcoxon) then the observed value should be less than the critical value.

Level of significance for two tailed test			
0.10	0.05	0.02	0.01
Level of significance for one tailed test			
0.05	0.025	0.01	0.005
N =			
1.000			
0.900	1.000	1.000	
0.829	0.886	0.943	1.000
0.714	0.786	0.893	0.929
0.643	0.738	0.833	0.881
0.600	0.700	0.783	0.883
0.564	0.648	0.745	0.794
0.536	0.618	0.709	0.755
0.503	0.587	0.671	0.727
0.484	0.560	0.648	0.703
0.464	0.538	0.622	0.675
0.443	0.521	0.604	0.654
0.429	0.503	0.582	0.635
0.414	0.485	0.566	0.615
0.401	0.472	0.550	0.600
0.391	0.460	0.535	0.584
0.380	0.447	0.520	0.570
0.370	0.435	0.508	0.556
0.361	0.425	0.496	0.544
0.353	0.415	0.486	0.532
0.344	0.406	0.476	0.521
0.337	0.398	0.466	0.511
0.331	0.390	0.457	0.501
0.324	0.382	0.448	0.491
0.317	0.375	0.440	0.483
0.312	0.368	0.433	0.475
0.306	0.362	0.425	0.467

The N values (leftmost column) are: 4, 5, 6, 7, 8, 9, 10, 11, 12, 13, 14, 15, 16, 17, 18, 19, 20, 21, 22, 23, 24, 25, 26, 27, 28, 29, 30.

Example of a critical value of Spearman's correlation

In this case, the observed value of *rho* must be equal to or larger than the critical values in the table for the result to be significant (reject the null hypothesis).

At this level of significance, there is a probability of 5% that the results were due to chance/error.

N = number of participants

These numbers are the critical values.

Factors affecting choice of statistical test

How to choose the correct statistical test? The choice of statistical test will depend on three main factors:

- **Research hypothesis** (are you testing for a difference or a correlation?)
- **Levels of measurement** (what type of data is it: nominal, ordinal, interval?)
- **Is the data related or unrelated?** (are the same participants or different participants being used?)

Research hypothesis

What is the research hypothesis trying to show? Is it looking for a ***difference*** in the sample of data collected from the two conditions? For example, in the hypothesis 'young males have more car accidents then young females', you are predicting a difference in driving between the two groups (teenage male and female drivers). Or is the research looking for a ***correlation*** (relationship) between a set of scores? For example, 'the older you get the more car accidents you have' (this is predicting a relationship between age and accidents).

Levels of measurement

The type of data collected in the study will determine the appropriate statistical test to use. The four different types of quantitative data that can be collected are nominal, ordinal, interval and ratio. They are known as **levels of measurements**.

- **Nominal data** involves recording results in *separate categories*. For example, a teacher may categorise which month each student was born (e.g. March or December). Each category is unrelated in as much as you can only be in one category (you can't be born in both March and December) so the data is also referred to as *non-continuous* data. There is no order of preference or rank of results, just separate categories.

- **Ordinal data** involves reordering the data in separate categories, but this time the categories are *ranked in order* according to the results. For example, we can rank the winner and runners-up in a singing contest in terms of first (Elena), second (Maria), third (Natasha), and so on. However, ordinal data does not tell us the *difference* between each result (category), in as much as we do not know how much better the winner was than the runners-up. Ordinal data does not allow us to compare the results.

- **Interval data,** like ordinal data, is ranked in order, but this time the distances (or intervals) between the ranked orders are *equal* to each other. For example, the number of days between the start of 1981 and 1982 is the same as those between 1983 and 1984 – namely 365 days. On a Fahrenheit temperature scale, the interval between 70 and 80 degrees is the same as that between 30 and 40 degrees – namely 10 degrees.

- **Ratio data** is the same as interval data, but for one difference – ratio data has an absolute true *zero point*. The zero point allows comparisons to be made, such as 'twice as much' or 'half as much'. For example, if you ask three students how rich they are, student A may have £100, student B may have £50 and student C may have £25. So we can say that student A is twice as rich as student B, and four times as rich as student C. This is possible because the scale starts at zero, which signifies nothing (no money). You can see how this compares to interval data by looking at the Fahrenheit temperature example – 0 degrees does not mean *no* temperature at all. It is not a genuine zero but a *false* zero, just a point on a scale (because there are more temperatures below zero!).

Related and unrelated data

Next you will need to see if you have related or unrelated data:

- **Unrelated data (independent measures):** the participants were used in only one condition (i.e. different participants were used for different conditions, never in two conditions). Each participant produces only one set of data which is usually then compared with another person's data.

- **Related data (repeated measures):** the same participants are used in all the conditions. This is so you can compare the score of each participant in one condition with their own performance in the other condition.

Choosing an Inferential Test

Are you testing for a difference?

Participant design	What type of data do you have? (Level of measurement)		
	Nominal Data	**Ordinal Data**	**Interval/Ratio Data**
Repeated measures or matched pairs	Sign test	Wilcoxon test	Related t-test
Independent groups	Chi-squared test	Mann-Whitney (U) test	Unrelated t-test

Are you testing for a correlation? (relationship)

Ordinal Data	**Interval/Ratio Data**
Spearman's test	Pearson's test

How to use the critical values table

To find the appropriate critical value in a table you will need to know:

- **Number of participants.** For the Spearman's Rho, Wilcoxon and Mann Whitney U you need to know the number of participants used in the group(s) study, which is written as 'N'. In studies using *independent group design* there are two values for N (one for each group of participants) called N1 and N2. For the Chi-squared test, you will also need to know the degree of freedom (df). This is calculated by the number of cells there are (number of rows in your table – 1) (number of columns in your table – 1). For example, if your table has 4 rows and 2 columns, the calculation for the df = (4-1)(2-1) =3. For a two by two table (two columns and two rows) df is 1 and for a three by two table df is 2.

- **One tailed or two tailed test.** If the research hypothesis was a directional hypothesis, then you use a one tailed test, if it was a non-directional you use a two tailed test.

- **Significance level.** What is the stated level of significance selected? (E.g. $p \leq 0.05$)

Exam Questions

1. A psychologist was interested in testing a new treatment for people with eating disorders. She put up adverts in several London clinics to recruit participants. Thirty people came forward and they were all given a structured interview by a trained therapist. The therapist then calculated a numerical score for each participant as a measure of their current functioning, where 50 indicated excellent, healthy functioning and zero indicated failure to function adequately. The psychologist then randomly allocated half the participants to a treatment group and half to a no-treatment group. After eight weeks, each participant was re assessed using a structured interview conducted by the same trained therapist, and given a new numerical score. The trained therapist did not know which participants had been in either group. For each participant, the psychologist calculated an improvement score by subtracting the score at the start of the study from the score after eight weeks. The greater the number, the better the improvement.

   The psychologist used a statistical test to find out if there was a significant difference in improvement between the 'treatment' and 'no-treatment' groups. She found a significant difference at the 5% level for a one-tailed test **(p≤ 0.05).**

	Treatment group	Non-treatment group
Median	10.9	2.7
Range	2.1	0.8

   What is the likelihood of the psychologist having made a Type 1 error in this study?
   Explain your answer. . . . . **(2 marks)**

2. A psychologist at the local university agrees to carry out a study to investigate the claim that eating a healthy breakfast improves reading skills. He has access to 400 five-year-old children from 10 local schools, and decides to use 100 children (50 in the experimental group and 50 in the control group). Since the children are so young, he needs to obtain parental consent for them to take part in his study.

   The psychologist asks some of his students to conduct a separate observational study at the same time on the same group of children. The aim of this observational study is to test the idea that eating a healthy breakfast affects playground behaviour.

   The psychologist used a Mann-Whitney test to analyse the data.
   Give two reasons why he chose this test. . . . . **(2 marks)**

www.ingramcontent.com/pod-product-compliance
Lightning Source LLC
Chambersburg PA
CBHW081229020426
42333CB00018B/2465